NONVIOLENT RESISTANCE AS A PHILOSOPHY OF LIFE

ALSO AVAILABLE FROM BLOOMSBURY

Gandhi and Philosophy, by Shaj Mohan and Divya Dwivedi
On Resistance, by Howard Caygill
Pacifism, by Robert L. Holmes
The Ethics of Nonviolence, by Robert L. Holmes
Transformative Pacifism, by Andrew Fiala

NONVIOLENT RESISTANCE AS A PHILOSOPHY OF LIFE

Gandhi's Enduring Relevance

RAMIN JAHANBEGLOO

BLOOMSBURY ACADEMIC
LONDON • NEW YORK • OXFORD • NEW DELHI • SYDNEY

BLOOMSBURY ACADEMIC
Bloomsbury Publishing Plc
50 Bedford Square, London, WC1B 3DP, UK
1385 Broadway, New York, NY 10018, USA

BLOOMSBURY, BLOOMSBURY ACADEMIC and the Diana logo are trademarks of Bloomsbury Publishing Plc

First published in Great Britain 2021

Cover design by Toby Way (tobyway.co.uk)
Cover photograph © AFP / Stringer / Getty Images

A catalogue record for this book is available from the British Library.

Library of Congress Cataloging-in-Publication Data
Names: Jahanbegloo, Ramin, author.
Title: Nonviolent resistance as a philosophy of life: Gandhi's enduring relevance / Ramin Jahanbegloo.
Description: London; New York: Bloomsbury Academic, 2021. | Includes bibliographical references and index.
Identifiers: LCCN 2020036936 (print) | LCCN 2020036937 (ebook) | ISBN 9781350168299 (hardback) | ISBN 9781350168282 (paperback) | ISBN 9781350168305 (ebook) | ISBN 9781350168312 (epub)
Subjects: LCSH: Government, Resistance to–History–20th century. | Civil disobedience–History–20th century. | Nonviolence–History–20th century.
Classification: LCC JC328.3 .J355 2021 (print) | LCC JC328.3 (ebook) | DDC 303.6/1–dc23
LC record available at https://lccn.loc.gov/2020036936
LC ebook record available at https://lccn.loc.gov/2020036937

ISBN: HB: 978-1-3501-6829-9
PB: 978-1-3501-6828-2
ePDF: 978-1-3501-6830-5
eBook: 978-1-3501-6831-2

Typeset by Deanta Global Publishing Services, Chennai, India

To find out more about our authors and books visit www.bloomsbury.com and sign up for our newsletters.

To my nonviolent friend
Roberto Toscano

Hatred is never appeased by hatred in this world. By non-hatred alone is hatred appeased. This is a law eternal.

The Buddha

CONTENTS

Introduction

An Idea Whose Time Has Come

This book is the outcome of thirty years of reflection and practice of nonviolence. But more precisely, it is the consequence and after-effect of political events and intellectual debates that marked our historical consciousness in the past 150 years. There is, however, another central reason to the publication of this book: simply that nonviolence is an idea whose time has come. Nonviolence is an art of organizing the society that bears no resemblance to whatever organizing methods preceded it. Anyone who studies the Indian independence movement or the American civil rights movement must acknowledge the novelty and originality of the nonviolent method formulated and put into action by Mohandas Karamchand Gandhi and Martin Luther King, Jr. Prophets of nonviolent resistance, both Gandhi and King rank among the greatest political strategists of all time. Gandhi and King have been successful, while continuing to be relevant, because they realized that nonviolent resistance is basically an idea whose time had come. They showed that nonviolence could be possible in a world gripped by the fear of violence. However, their search for a deeper meaning of nonviolence as a philosophy of life, rather than simply a method of social action was (is) not an easy task for the simple man on the street. What Gandhi and King realized through their readings of Buddha, Jesus, Tolstoy and many other grand peacemakers of history was that nonviolence is not only a strategic option, but also a philosophical choice, vital to the existence and moral progress of humankind. As Gandhi once said, the point here is not merely to change the world, but to change oneself in order to keep one's commitment to nonviolence.

Unlike Machiavelli, Gandhi knew that there is no sure path to the political organization of the society. But he also knew that the nonviolent method of resistance and change could be extraordinarily effective and successful if it was combined with truth- seeking. 'Truth and Nonviolence', wrote Gandhi in *Young India*, 'are perhaps [the most active] forces you have in the world. . . . They reside in the human breast, and they are actively working their way whether you are awake or whether you are asleep, whether you are walking leisurely or playing an active game. The panoplied warrior of Truth and Nonviolence is ever and incessantly active.'[1] We should not forget that Gandhi's greatest contribution to the theory of politics was the concept of *Satyagraha*, which means literarily 'grasping the truth' (Satya+ agraha). Formulated during his campaigns in South Africa, *Satyagraha* was defined as the method of nonviolent resistance. Gandhi understood and theorized nonviolence as a mode of upholding truth. As such, what Gandhi is saying is that remaining loyal to truth is beneficial to oneself and to the other. Maybe that is why, for Gandhi, 'there is no such thing as defeat in nonviolent resistance'.[2] But nonviolence is not always considered by our age as a win-win process. Many social activists who are fighting today against climate change or for peace may find the Gandhian working for truth an arduous enterprise. The reason is simple: Gandhian nonviolence is not a sprint, but a marathon. It needs long-distance runners who can make it to the finishing line. Gandhi defined nonviolence as 'soul force'. In other words, nonviolent social and political action introduced a new approach to the concept of power into human history. It combined the quest for spiritual truth with the struggle for organizing a just and compassionate society. Gandhi attempted to spiritualize politics by reconciling political power with higher principles of morality. The genius of Gandhi lay not in replacing the thermodynamics of power with the moral stature of sainthood, but in transforming political power from an end to a means for ethical transformation of the society. As a matter of fact, nonviolent thinkers like Henry David Thoreau, Leo Tolstoy and Mahatma Gandhi defined and practised politics beyond matters of government policy. Thoreau's famous statement 'that government is best which governs least'[3] inspired both Gandhi and King. Gandhi acknowledged Thoreau by adding that 'When people come into possession of political power, the interference with the freedom of the people is reduced to a minimum. In other words, a nation that runs its affairs smoothly and effectively without such State interference is truly democratic. Where such a condition is absent, the form of government is democratic in name.'[4]

Gandhi, like Thoreau and Tolstoy, saw nonviolence as the work of civil society and not the state. The three of them believed that violence was more the work of the state rather than that of civil society. That is why a thinker like Tolstoy considered the state as an institutionalized form of violence. As Tolstoy says, because of the very structure of the state, one who wants to reach its apex needs to seize power and to retain it with violence. In other words, one can rule the state if and only if one transgresses the most basic principles of ethics. According to Tolstoy,

> All men in power assert that their authority is necessary to keep bad men from doing violence to the good, thus assuming that they themselves are the good who protect others from the bad. But ruling means using force, and using force means doing what the man subjected to violence does not wish done, and to which the perpetrator would certainly object if the violence were applied to himself. Therefore to rule means to do to others what we would not have done to ourselves – that is, doing wrong.[5]

We can find Tolstoy's critique of the state as a violent and authoritarian mechanism in Gandhi's insight that nonviolent power can be expressed more by an ethical and self-disciplined civil society than by a self-centred state that acts through coercive power. Thus, on political grounds, Gandhi, like Tolstoy, settled for a minimal state or a stateless society. For Gandhi, nonviolence, as an ethical and spiritual destiny for humankind, was ultimately incompatible with the institution of the state and the modern theory of political power. Though he did not see any contradiction between the political and the spiritual, his call to humanity was to shake itself out of its self-inflicted unethical lust for power. For Gandhi, nonviolent resistance was a civic virtue which went hand in hand with an ethical engagement in public life. As Granville Austin wrote in his seminal political history of the Indian Constitution, 'Gandhi believed that the achievement of social justice as the common lot must proceed from a character reformation of each individual, from the heart and mind of each Indian outward into society as a whole. The impetus for reform must not come downward from government, and a reformed society would need no government to regulate or control it.'[6] This certainly does not mean that Gandhi considered nonviolent action akin to arm-chair resistance. On the contrary, Gandhi and many other theorists of nonviolent resistance believed that an individual who did not actively participate in the public space could not be counted as a practitioner of nonviolence. There was no ambiguity whatsoever about his stand on the matter.

For Gandhi, as for King, the only way to experiment with truth was in the public space. Moreover, nonviolence, as an experiment with truth, makes sense only in a world of interconnected souls. As Hannah Arendt puts it correctly, the public space is the realm of speech and action.

> The point is, rather, that we know from experience that no one can adequately grasp the objective world in its full reality all on his own, because the world always shows and reveals itself to him from only one perspective, which corresponds to his standpoint in the world and is determined by it. If someone wants to see and experience the world as it 'really' is, he can do so only by understanding it as something that is shared by many people, lies between them, separates and links them, showing itself differently to each and comprehensible only to the extent that many people can talk about it and exchange their opinions and perspectives with one another, over against one another. Only in the freedom of our speaking with one another does the world, as that about which we speak, emerge in its objectivity and visibility from all sides.[7]

Arendt would certainly not have approved of Tolstoy, Gandhi and King in their spiritual attitude towards nonviolence as a political action, since she considered the political world as an expression of human plurality and not as a divine creation. Nevertheless, for Arendt, nonviolent action, like any other political action, would be the direct consequence of the political promise inherent in human plurality. To speak in Arendtian terms, nonviolence occurs between human beings, and so quite outside God's creation. But Arendt made a further point that shows her differences with nonviolent thinkers like Gandhi, King and the Dalai Lama. She affirmed: 'In a head-on clash between violence and power, the outcome is hardly in doubt. If Gandhi's enormously powerful and successful strategy of nonviolent resistance had met with a different enemy – Stalin's Russia, Hitler's Germany, even prewar Japan, instead of England – the outcome would not have been decolonization, but massacre and submission.'[8] However, unlike a philosopher like Jean-Paul Sartre, Arendt knew clearly that violence is not creative and does not 'create' free men. By saying so, Arendt was well aware that the real antithesis was not between violence and nonviolence, but between power and violence. The opening section of the second part of her famous essay titled *On Violence* starts with a quote from the American sociologist, C. Wright Mills, who bluntly declares that 'All politics is a struggle for power; the ultimate kind of power is violence.'[9] But while rejecting this conception of power, as a form of ruling over individuals or groups, Arendt brings our attention to the fact that the rule of violence would bring the end of power as 'the human ability to act in concert'.[10] In the eyes of Arendt, power is, therefore, by definition anti-violent or nonviolent, in the sense that violence has an anti-political essence. As she emphasizes, 'Violence can always destroy power; out of the barrel of a gun grows the most effective command, resulting in the most instant and perfect obedience. What never can grow out of it is power.'[11] However, Arendt is well aware of the fact that violence and power have together accompanied many historical events, especially during revolutionary times. But according to Richard Bernstein, if we understand correctly how Arendt defines violence and power, 'we can appreciate why she separates politics from violence – why merging them is an obfuscating confusion. Violence, although it can be lethal, is mute; it is instrumental. But power requires speech and articulation'.[12] However, Arendt never studied nonviolent resistance as a legitimate form of political action. Moreover, even though she declared that violence is never legitimate, she acknowledged that 'there are circumstances in which violence can be justified'.[13]

Surprisingly, even as an acute and attentive analyst of the American society, Arendt's conceptions of political pluralism never truly focused on the political project of the American civil rights movement and, more specifically, on the nonviolent struggle of Martin Luther King, Jr. As wrong as Arendt might be on so many of the particulars of the situation in the American civil rights movement and in relation to the true philosophical significance of the Gandhian nonviolence, her views stood as a warning about too facile a version of dismissing nonviolence as an irrelevant mode of political thought. As such, Arendt's strict distinction between politics and morality, as well as her critique of the moralism of political views beyond the proper limits of politics, brought her to dismiss nonviolence as a way of moralizing politics, though she perceives it as a tool in the process of constituting or perpetuating freedom in the public sphere. Unlike Gandhi, King, the Dalai Lama and many other representatives of principled nonviolence, for a political theorist like Arendt, the ethics of compassion was of no political significance. Unlike Gandhi, King and the Dalai Lama who derive political decision-making from the primacy of the ethical over the political, Arendt makes it clear in her book *On Revolution* that the ethics of compassion is of no political significance. According to her, because

> Compassion abolishes the distance, the worldly space between men where political matters, the whole realm of human affairs, are located, it remains, politically speaking, irrelevant and without consequence. . . . As a rule it is not compassion which sets out to change worldly conditions in order to ease human suffering, but if it does, it will shun the drawn-out wearisome processes of persuasion, negotiation and compromise, which are the processes of law and politics, and lend its voice to the suffering itself, which must claim for swift and direct action, that is, for action with the means of violence.[14]

Gandhian nonviolence and its relevance for today's world cannot be acknowledged without a clear reference to Mahatma Gandhi's idea of all-encompassing compassion and his spirit of service to humankind. Gandhi's emphasis on the importance and priority of moral legitimacy of political power provided the foundation of a new approach to the problem of politics. Not until Gandhi was assassinated and his legacy of nonviolent action was reconfirmed and revitalized by Martin Luther King, Jr. in the 1960s in America did the political theorists accept the view that in Gandhian philosophy politics is a means to some higher end. This nonviolent conception of politics, in which the central idea was to limit the sphere of government as far as was possible and necessary in order to empower the powerless victims of oppression and injustice, contributed significantly in healing the destructive human divisions around the world and launched the global disciplined mass movements for peace and plurality. However, as Gene Sharp says, 'We need to remember that Gandhi was no naïve playing at politics, imagining the world to be one of sweet harmony, gentleness, and love. The times in which he lived and worked had many of the characteristics of our own times. Those characteristics include the existence of acute conflicts, dictatorships, great violence, mass killings, and communal and racial hatreds. We often forget that Gandhi was tough and realistic. He fully recognized the role of power in political conflicts. Indeed, it seems that he understood power far better than those leaders of today who dogmatically believe that violence and military might are the only real source of political and international power.'[15]

In Gandhi's design of nonviolent action, it was not freedom (as in the Arendtian meaning of politics) but the empowerment of the weakest which was fundamental. That is why, in his conception of politics, Gandhi did not differentiate between ends and means. From the Gandhian perspective of nonviolent resistance, what the means of action have in common with the ends is that they are both not judged and taken into account according to the expediency, but in relation to the primacy of the ethical over the political. For Gandhi, as for Martin Luther King, Jr., nonviolence is both a means and an end. Of course, we all know that for Mahatma Gandhi, nonviolence, as the art of empowering the powerless, was not just about liberal tolerance and participation in periodic elections, but mainly about affirming the right to dissent. As such, Gandhian nonviolence gave rise to nonviolence as a new manner of mind and a new order of values. Maybe that is why even after more than seventy years, the Gandhian philosophy of nonviolence has remained the greatest weapon in the armoury of dissenters, from Nelson Mandela's South Africa to Lech Walesa's Poland, to Martin Luther King, Jr.'s America and to protestors in Algeria, Iran and Hong Kong. If there is only one message for which Gandhian Satyagraha should be remembered, it is the habit of questioning the reality of the world without necessarily taking it for granted. The core idea of Gandhi's philosophy of nonviolent resistance, which we find repeated with Martin Luther King, Jr., Nelson Mandela, Vaclav Havel and many other dissenters round the globe, is that one should not extend one's obedience to people in power without testing the viability of their authority on ethical grounds. According to Gandhi, 'Even the most despotic government cannot stand except for the consent of the governed which consent is often forcibly procured by the despot. Immediately the subject ceases to fear the despotic force, his power is gone.'[16] As we can see, in Gandhian nonviolent resistance, the citizen keeps a constant vigil over those who wield power and have a tendency to slip into authoritarian violence. So, the ultimate allegiance of a citizen is not towards the state, but towards his/her moral conscience. Gandhi's touchstone for nonviolent resistance was one's inner voice, the guiding light that enlightens one's conscience in the process of confrontation with injustice and evil. The choice of nonviolent dissent, thus, becomes a strategy to contest autocracy, and also a moral duty of the citizen to ensure the well-being of the political. One can find herein a bridge between politics and ethics, as the latter becomes a soul force to examine the truth of the former. Maybe we need to come back here to the two concepts of 'empathy' and 'compassion', which were dismissed as a-political by Hannah Arendt, as the two ethical pillars of Gandhian nonviolent resistance.

What an intercultural analysis of the Gandhian nonviolence reveals to us is that unlike much of contemporary liberal political thinking, which puts rights before duties, empathy and cross-cultural understanding are the hallmarks of the Gandhian view of everyday politics. At the heart of Gandhi's ethics of empathy is looking within oneself in regard to the otherness of the Other, changing oneself and then changing the world. That is to say, at a more fundamental level, for Gandhi, cultures and nations are not isolated entities because they all play a special role in the nonviolent making of human history. Therefore, Gandhi rarely speaks in terms of linear world history. His goal for every culture (including his own) is the same as his goal for every individual: to experiment with Truth. This is a way to open up the world to a transformative dialogue among cultures. Therefore, at a more philosophical level, in Gandhian nonviolent resistance, every culture should learn from others. As a result, politics for Gandhi is a matter of nonviolent organization of society with the aim of becoming more mature and more truthful. At the same time, Gandhi is always concerned with developing cooperation among nations in terms of mutual understanding, empathic friendship and nonviolent partnership. Gandhian nonviolent resistance is a constant experimentation with modes of border-crossing and otherness. This is why Gandhi affirms, 'I do not want my house to be walled in on sides and my windows to be stuffed. I want the cultures of all the lands to be blown about my house as freely as possible. But I refuse to be blown off my feet by any.'[17] This statement of Gandhi's has a particular relevance to the practice of nonviolence in our globalized world. Gandhi's metaphor of the 'house' can be understood as a decentralized self-governed system. This is where nonviolent partnership accompanied by empathic friendship can take place among equally respected and equally valid cultures. As a result, Gandhi's ethics of nonviolence is deeply rooted in a dialogical approach to politics as an art of organizing a community of human beings with compassion. Interestingly, we can find the Gandhian tradition of thought rethought and re-evaluated by Martin Luther King, Jr. in his concept of 'world house'. King's idea was that nonviolent resistance can take us to a level of ontological transformation, where beyond the logic of class, race and religion there would be a path towards the fulfilment of the promise of empathy and compassion in the modern society. Self-determination and community were inseparable in the thought of Dr King. However, the self was always related to the other, and no one could experience his/her self in total solitude. 'We are made to live together', King underlines, 'because of the interrelated structure of reality.'[18] For King, the universal human dignity was shared by all individuals. Therefore, King considered nonviolent resistance as a political act for the sake of the dignity of the human personality and the ideal of a dialogical and compassionate community. Like Gandhi, King was also aware of 'willingness to suffer' as a moral requirement in a nonviolent struggle. According to Gandhi,

> Things of fundamental importance to the people are not secured through reason alone, but have to be purchased with their suffering. . . . Suffering is infinitely more powerful than the law of the jungle for converting the opponent and opening his ears, which are otherwise shut, to the voice of reason. Nobody has probably

drawn up more petitions or espoused more forlorn causes than I, and I have come to this fundamental conclusion that, if you want something really important to be done, you must not merely satisfy the reason, you must move the heart also. The appeal of reason is more to the head, but the penetration of the heart comes from suffering. It opens up the inner understanding in man. Suffering is the badge of the human race, not the sword.[19]

The point here is that in Gandhian nonviolent resistance the experience of suffering is closely related to modes of participation in common concerns and community-engendering values. It takes place in the public sphere, in the realm of political talk and action, and not in solitude. Nonviolence is not something that can be built, but it is something that can be performed and observed. Thus, self-suffering as a nonviolent weapon is a rich and fascinating public performance which lights up the dark corners of human nature. In the words of Martin Luther King, Jr.: 'The method of nonviolence is based on the conviction that the universe is on the side of justice. It is this deep faith in the future that causes the nonviolent resister to accept suffering without retaliation.'[20] As we can see the starting point of King's philosophy of nonviolence, as well as his final vision, is not only redemptive but also transformative, continuously manifested through his thinking and action. King, like Gandhi, saw the relation among human beings rooted in the search for Truth. In an interview he gave to *Playboy* magazine, King underlined that one 'of the major strengths of the nonviolent weapon is its strange power to transform and transmute the individuals who subordinate themselves to its disciplines, investing them with a cause that is larger than themselves'.[21] From King's point of view, as from that of Gandhi, the space that exists between a nonviolent resister and his/her opponent in a nonviolent struggle cannot, of course, be without pain and suffering. 'The nonviolent resister is willing to accept violence if necessary, but never to inflict it,' King writes. 'Suffering, the nonviolent resister realizes, has tremendous educational and transforming possibilities'.[22] In other words, at the centre of the problematic of nonviolence stands the principle of empathy. Viewed from this vantage point the question arises whether politics and empathy are at all compatible, or whether politics does not begin precisely where empathy ends. If we ask here in all seriousness about the limitations of nonviolence, there is no doubt that Gandhian nonviolence, as the politicization of the space of empathy between individuals, marks indeed a new understanding of the otherness of the Other in the human community. Nonviolence begins when human beings start comprehending and moving in the world in a distinctly compassionate way, by living in truth. But frankly, what is missing today in world politics, even in our liberal democracies, is politics with compassion. Politics with conscience is not the pure practice of morality; it is mostly the creation of a space that should be understood in terms of decency and nonviolence. It is simply a matter of serving 'the otherness of others'. This is a conception of responsibility that certainly does not correspond to those who stand on the side of power and a centralized state, but it concretely concerns the lives of those who think differently and want to live autonomously. This genuine concern for the otherness of others reminds us of the inherent fragility of human existence and of the frailty of the human political condition.

What nonviolent movements around the world have shown us for the past hundred years, starting with Mahatma Gandhi and ending with the student movement in Hong Kong, is that nonviolent revolution, unlike the classical revolutions, is not only a political revolution, but also what Martin Luther King, Jr. called a 'revolution of values'. King considered history as a matter of listening and learning. He knew that without choosing to listen to each other, humans will walk in the dark. King won his wager, not because he defeated his opponents through physical strength, but because he was of the opinion that human dignity matters. After all, combining politics and ethics is not a naïve dream. Naturally, for those who understand politics as a heightened responsibility for the ethical state of society, subordinating politics to moral conscience is to understand and practise democracy in terms of decency. If that is the case, it is time for citizens of this world to become aware of the fact that there is only one way in the world to remain faithful to the nonviolent notion of politics: to be decent and to act in harmony with one's moral conscience. Looking back over the last 100 years in world political history, especially since the movements led by moral leaders like Gandhi, King, Mandela, Mother Teresa, Havel, the Dalai Lama and many others, we see the growing influence and impact of nonviolent struggle. Victor Hugo once remarked: 'You can resist an invading army; you cannot resist an idea whose time has come.' Today nonviolence is just such an idea. Money, power, armies are incapable of keeping nonviolence from being unleashed once again as a global idea. From a universal perspective, political peace on earth and the survival of the planet are the two most important issues of the twenty-first century. From an individual perspective, giving meaning to one's life and finding a dignified place in the human community are the two things that can empower each one of us. But, once again, it all begins with a process of questioning. No civilization can live without practising the art of questioning, even less a civilization like ours, which is living through a global challenge and a planetary crisis. An appeal to the Gandhian philosophy of resistance would bring back the question of questioning to our everyday social and political grammar. Here, nonviolent resistance is made possible by an implicit questioning of the social and political institutions. Therefore, from a Gandhian perspective, critique of the political represents a challenge to the idea of politics as power. This is where nonviolent experiments with the political can be regarded not only as a form of interconnecting the political and the ethical, but also as a means of inverting the key principles of modern political thought which dismisses empathic friendship in the name of the guarantee of individual liberties in the private sphere. As basic as it is in Gandhi's philosophy of nonviolent resistance, empathic friendship is not only a right to be free, but also a mode of political selfhood. We can find herein the reference to the Gandhian questioning of the political, followed by the nonviolent conception of self-awareness and consciousness of one's political obligations towards others. Nonviolent transformation of the society and its values is, therefore, tied to the self-transformative nature of the politics of nonviolence. This brings us to the inherent instability of democratic rule in our world and its capacity to give birth to populism. If this populist claim to rule becomes inseparable from majoritarianism, particularly in liberal societies, it is a heavy recipe for minority vulnerability and ethical deficit. For Gandhi, populist political action came with a host of dangers, among them the rise of the mobs. Gandhi's response was to return moral capital and enlightened questioning to the dynamics of mass action. The latter could work not through the sheer force of numbers, but through the empathic cooperation of morally conscious individuals. This was one of the most innovative features of Gandhian nonviolent politics. As a matter of fact, the challenge for the future of our world is to be able to exploit the remarkable political efficacy of Gandhian nonviolent resistance without moralizing nonviolent politics. After all, the legacy of Gandhian nonviolence for nonviolent movements in today's world is that attentiveness to questions of individual egoism, populism, moral hubris and authoritarian power should make us understand that nonviolent action which aims to undo the legitimacy of existing institutions must also generate new modes of individual and collective self-rule to redefine and reconstitute the art of the political.

1

The Limits of Violence

We are all concerned with violence throughout our lives, but strangely there is no consensus about the concept of violence. Some advocate it as a form of liberation from tyranny. Others reject it as a destructive instrument in the hands of those who want to practise their power over the others. But the crucial question that can be of great importance to our contemporary discussions on violence is what we can learn from the thinkers of violence about the role of this concept in the real world. As we saw in the introduction, a thinker like Hannah Arendt who tries to study the antithetical relation between power and violence finds herself closer to 'an idealized conception of the Greek polis that never really existed',[1] than to Gandhian or Kingian ideas of nonviolent organization of society. However, Arendt was not a supporter of violence, and when she wrote her book *On Violence*, she was responding to Frantz Fanon's book *The Wretched of the Earth*. Fanon's work is a critique of colonial violence, but at the same time he tries to justify the necessity of the liberating violence against the colonial system. Fanon argues that violence has an emancipatory role; that is why some of his interpreters[2] have called Fanon's concept of violence a 'nonviolent violence'. However, Fanon himself considers the notion of violence, in a Marxian–Hegelian manner, as a dialectical necessity. According to Emmanuel Hansen, the reason

> that Fanon advances to justify his argument for the emancipatory role of violence is that it is the colonizer who initially introduces violence into the relationship between the settler and the native. We are not told the origin of the settler's violence. Presumably, it is part and parcel of the capitalist society, where alienation is the feature of each person's life and where each person treats the other as an object. The violence of the colonizer is used not only to exploit the material wealth of the colonies but to dehumanize the native. The initial violence of the settler is the thesis, and here one has to remember that, according to Fanon, the initial contact between the settler and the native is always marked by violence. This violence of the settler creates an antithesis, the violence of the native, but against himself. For some time the native turns the violence on himself, but then a point is reached 'when daily life becomes impossible.' The native then responds to the settler's violence with violence.[3]

In his book *Violence: Thinking without Banisters*, Richard Bernstein explains the essence of Fanon's arguments clearly and distinctly in the following terms:

> Most of *The Wretched of the Earth* is not about the violence of the colonized; it is about the obstacles that stand in the way of achieving liberation.... Indigenous peoples only become colonized under the colonial system; and it is the inhuman abuses of the colonizers that spur the spontaneous violence of the colonized. This spontaneous

violence has to be channeled and limited; it has to be directed into a disciplined armed struggle. Otherwise it leads to disintegration and self-defeat. This requires a leadership that listens to the people and is responsive to their needs. Armed struggle is required, Fanon argues, because colonial systems – especially in Africa – will use any means they can to preserve the colonial system.[4]

It goes without saying that revolutionary decolonization is a justified form of violence for Fanon. As he asserts in his famous book *The Wretched of the Earth*,

> Violence alone, perpetrated by the people, violence organized and guided by the leadership, provides the key for the masses to decipher social reality. Without this struggle, without this praxis there is nothing but a carnival parade and a lot of hot air. All that is left is a slight re-adaptation, a few reforms at the top, a flag, and down at the bottom a shapeless, writhing mass, still mired in the Dark Ages.[5]

Although Fanon uses the word 'violence' very frequently, he does not give his reader a clear definition of this concept. In fact, in Fanon's system of thought *violence* and *force* become interchangeable. Moreover, Fanon clearly rejects nonviolence, because he thinks that nonviolence preserves colonialism. According to Emmanuel B. Eyo and Amambo Edung Essien, 'Fanon dismissed the philosophy of non-violence as popularized by Mahatma Gandhi and Martin Luther King Jr. He sees all nonviolent appeals as a distraction of the colonized and admonishes them to continue in the search for a new humanity through the only possible way which is violence.'[6]

If Fanon had lived longer and had witnessed Nelson Mandela's release from prison followed by his election as the first black president of South Africa, he would have certainly disagreed with Mandela on the nonviolent process of negotiation and reconciliation between the blacks and the whites in the making of a new South Africa. The reason is simple and this is one of the fantasies of the violent theories of politics and society: they are all eschatological and utopian. Arendt also wrote serious critiques about Fanon's theory of violence and its transformative power. As she explains in her book *On Violence*,

> Not many authors of rank glorified violence for violence's sake; but these few – Sorel, Pareto, Fanon – were motivated by a much deeper hatred of bourgeois society and were led to a much more radical break with its moral standards than the conventional Left, which was chiefly inspired by compassion and a burning desire for justice. To tear the mask of hypocrisy from the face of the enemy, to unmask him and the devious machinations and manipulations that permit him to rule without using violent means, that is, to provoke action even at the risk of annihilation so that the truth may come out – these are still among the strongest motives in today's violence on the campuses and the streets.[7]

We can now more fully appreciate Arendt's critique of Fanon, since she categorically rejects the idea that liberation from a colonial system or an oppressive regime is automatically accompanied by public freedom. However, unlike Arendt, for whom the crucial question of politics is to act under the human condition of plurality, Fanon considers political action as an answer to the question: 'Who is the source of control that can determine someone to do this rather than that?' For

Fanon, armed struggle is the only way to overthrow a colonial regime. But there is always the danger of regression to mass murder replacing the liberation process. As Bernstein emphasizes, 'Fanon is fully aware of the limits of violence in the fight against colonialism. Hatred and gratuitous barbarity by themselves fail to achieve liberation; they actually undermine the struggle for liberation.'[8]

Human beings can act together either to practise or to overcome systematic violence. This is a matter of the degree of intervention of the ethical in the political. As such, the question of the limits of violence is directly linked with the idea of political judgement and evaluation of the achievements of nonviolent power. There are moments in history when humanity used violence to save itself from the grips of violence, but to save humanity one cannot end violence with counterviolence. As Martin Luther King, Jr. emphasizes,

I've seen too much hate to want to hate, myself, and every time I see it, I say to myself, hate is too great a burden to bear. Somehow we must be able to stand up against our most bitter opponents and say: 'We shall match your capacity to inflict suffering by our capacity to endure suffering. We will meet your physical force with soul force. Do to us what you will and we will still love you. We cannot in all good conscience obey your unjust laws and abide by the unjust system, because non-cooperation with evil is as much a moral obligation as is cooperation with good, so throw us in jail and we will still love you. Bomb our homes and threaten our children, and, as difficult as it is, we will still love you. Send your hooded perpetrators of violence into our communities at the midnight hour and drag us out on some wayside road and leave us half-dead as you beat us, and we will still love you. Send your propaganda agents around the country and make it appear that we are not fit, culturally and otherwise, for integration, but we'll still love you. But be assured that we'll wear you down by our capacity to suffer, and one day we will win our freedom. We will not only win freedom for ourselves; we will appeal to your heart and conscience that we will win you in the process, and our victory will be a double victory.'[9]

What King shows us is that we need to invest in nonviolence like we invest in saving the environment. There is an urgent need to prevent the escalation of violence in our world. Unfortunately, in the eyes of many around the world, our age is considered as the age of violence, because representations of real or imagined violence are fused together and also because we have become intellectually passive and conformist in thinking nonviolence. Though it is clear that nonviolence cannot be absolute, one can argue that without the process of thinking the limits of violence, societies and communities will be unable to understand and practise political responsibility, especially in a democratic arena.

There are compelling reasons to limit violence and practise nonviolence, and yet at the same time humanity needs to acknowledge that there are exceptional circumstances (like Nazism) in which violence is justified. In such cases, the decisive challenge for humanity would be to remain truthful to the ethical while being responsible to the political. This is an urgent need which is also the beginning of a structural consideration. The limits of violence do not start with violence itself. They start with the moral values embraced and practised by the shared values of nonviolence. As such, what stands at the heart of the process of the taming of violence in the twenty-first century is a minimum ethics for dialogue and coexistence among cultures and traditions. When differences in values are seen in this context, it is not difficult for the East and the West to come up with a modus operandi of relating to each other while still respecting each other's cultures and traditions. As such, the politics of mutual recognition cannot go without certain common minimum values which serve as a starting point for humanity's moral coexistence and dialogue on this planet. This is accompanied by a deepening sense of a global human responsibility. This is a responsibility which could confront all the major issues of today's civilization. In order to have a deepening moral progress of humanity next to the technological progress and the advancement of instrumental rationality, humanity needs to feel responsible for the biosphere and towards the biosphere. It is this sense of belonging to the world and the responsibility which goes with it that seems to be pressing all cultures and religious traditions ever closer together. Without this sense of belonging to the world, 'all our pride in what we can do', says Hannah Arendt, 'will disappear into some kind of mutation of the human race; the whole of technology, seen from this point, in fact no longer appears "as the result of a conscious human effort to extend man's material powers, but rather a large-scale biological process."'[10] Once again, nonviolence is the key word here. However, nonviolence does not mean tolerating the conquest of the Earth or the destruction of the world. On the contrary, nonviolence is an active and responsible resistance against evil. In other words, limiting violence is not excusing away radical evil. Auschwitz, Gulag, the Cambodian Killing Fields, Rwanda and so on are good examples. By far the simplest explanation for all these atrocities and many others is that there is no limit to human violence. But how can humanity choose nonviolence as the paradigm for human coexistence, while taming the violence which persists in its choices and actions? If we take nonviolence as a serious choice in the global context, we should not be surprised that the end of violence is also located in the manner we consider the otherness of the Other. That is to say, nonviolence is the generic constituent for any dialogical rules of civility and decency. Only a truly moral conception of citizenship, which listens to the other with empathy and which learns from the past can reverse the meaninglessness and thoughtlessness of the de-civilizing process we are currently going through. The truth is that most of the barbarities in the world are sustained in the name of a reductionist view of civilization and humanity. Here we have the total absence of the empathic listening to the other. But we should never forget that the very condition of plurality for human beings is the empowerment of individuals as a vital element for the promotion of dialogue. Therefore, pluralist dialogue and empathic friendship can only be guaranteed in a society where every member gives up the use of violence. A nonviolent community, what Martin Luther King, Jr. called a 'Beloved Community', is, thus, a community that brings its members into a condition of dialogue and civility. Before that can happen, a culture of nonviolence needs to be encouraged and promoted among the members of each community. This is a necessary condition for challenging the grains of fanaticism, prejudice and hatred that hide in the barrels of particular traditions. So long as nonviolence is thus held prisoner by cultures of intolerance rejecting the otherness of the Other, the culture of violence will have the upper hand in our common world. As a matter of fact, the limits of violence can be prescribed only and only if humanity becomes conscious of the fact that the end of human history is not conquest of the planet and domination of all living creatures, but recognition and coexistence of all forms of life. Here, nonviolence is the key to a responsible and conscientious form of interconnectedness. Martin Luther King, Jr. gave us the best portrait of this interdependence. He wrote:

> All men are interdependent. Every nation is an heir of the vast treasury of ideas and labor to which both the living and the dead of all nations have contributed. Whether we realize it or not, each of us lives eternally 'in the red'. We are everlasting debtors to known and unknown men and women. When we arise in the morning, we go into the bathroom where we reach for sponge which was provided for us by a Pacific islander. We reach for soap that is created for us by a European. Then at the table we drink coffee which is proved for us by a South American, or tea by a Chinese or cocoa by a West African. Before we leave for our jobs we are already beholden to more than half of the world.[11]

As King observed, peace and companionship will not come out of a clash of arms, but out of compassionate justice lived and practised by nonviolent resisters and dissenters in the face of odds. Unquestionably this was also the essence of Albert Camus' critique of violence. Maybe that is why Camus' readers can discern in his work a special attention to the otherness of the Other as a shared sense of common dignity. Camus is not a Gandhian in the strict sense of the term, but he is very much concerned with the question of evil and a moral resistance against it. He, therefore, comes to the difficult philosophical position that the otherness of the Other can only be honoured by a genuine responsibility and resistance in the face of evil. As he writes in his *Fourth Letter to a German Friend,*

> I continue to believe that this world has no ultimate meaning. But I know that something in it has a meaning and that is man, because he is the only creature to insist on having one. This world has at least the truth of man, and our task is to provide its justification against fate itself. And it has no justification but man; hence he must be saved if we want to save the idea we have of life.[12]

Camus considered what he called the 'Meridian philosophy' or the 'New Mediterranean Culture' as a moment of clarity and lucidity to fight the radical evil of history. Camus defined the Mediterranean as a moment of measuredness (*la mesure*) and moral creativity. This is why he attributed a positive character to the revolt against evil as what he called a solar thought (*une pensée solaire*). Indeed, what Camus is seeking in his 'solar thought' is a critique of political or, more clearly, revolutionary violence. In a letter to D'Astier de la Vigerie in response to a criticism of his essay *Neither Victims nor Executioners,* he affirms: 'I have a horror of comfortable violence; I have a horror of those whose words exceed their actions. It is in this respect that I distance myself from certain of our great minds, for whose appeals to murder I will cease feeling contempt only when they themselves take up the executioner's gun.'[13] Of course, Camus is making reference here to Jean-Paul Sartre's preface to Frantz Fanon's *The Wretched of the Earth,* where he declares:

> [Fanon] shows perfectly clearly that this irrepressible violence is neither a storm in a teacup nor the re-emergence of savage instincts

nor even a consequence of resentment: it is man reconstructing himself. . . . When the peasants lay hands on a gun, the old myths fade, and one by one the taboos are overturned: a fighter's weapon is his humanity. For in the first phase of the revolt killing is a necessity: killing a European is killing two birds with one stone, eliminating in one go oppressor and the oppressed: leaving one man dead and the other man free.[14]

Camus' critique of Sartre's defence of violence is at the same time a way of analyzing and overcoming the Sartrean–Fanonian messianic vision of revolution, which gives way to the revolutionary dream of perfecting an imperfect world. Camus' understanding of the limits of violence goes hand in hand with his idea of 'compassionate justice' where there is a humanistic effort towards empathy and comprehension of the otherness of the Other. Camus' finality, therefore, is to arrive at a measured resistance against evil by discarding all forms of ideological and eschatological violence. That is to say, for Camus, human solidarity is based upon the negation of violence, and the negation of violence, in its turn, can only find its justification in this solidarity. As Camus insists, there can be no ethical understanding of human history without any reference to the generating values of solidarity and compassion.

Camus' radical deconstruction of the nature of violence in history and his emphasis on the role of compassion in justice find many points of convergence with the ethics of the other in the philosophy of Emmanuel Levinas. Levinas' claim to locate transcendence in the face of the Other resonates well with the problematic of the limits of violence as discussed in this chapter. Considering that Levinas assumes ethics as being prior to ontology, his philosophy seems to be a fruitful path to place the self in a posture of empathy and responsibility and to limit violence in the political realm. As Victoria Tahmasebi-Birgani deduces,

> For Levinas, the other is inassimilable and irreducible to the same; the otherness of the other is precisely the core of its singularity and of its humanity, over and above the rights she shares with the rest of humanity. The absolute alterity of the other is not the result of a fall but is in fact the nucleus of her humanity. Levinas' ethics demands that one be infinitely and irreplaceably responsible not merely for the other, but for her irreducible alterity.[15]

Levinas, like Camus, is not interested in the biological and psychological origins of violence. Levinas' work consists in exploring the ontological horizon of violence, by suggesting that the fact of being rooted in existence constitutes the drama of not being able to escape from it. Levinas very often uses terms such as 'the Same' (*le Meme*) and 'the Other' (*l'Autre*). According to him, the ego in its sameness is monopolistic and totalitizing, while the Other in its alterity is closely associated with the infinite. For Levinas, in opposition to the tradition of German idealism, 'morality begins when freedom, instead of being justified by itself, feels itself to be arbitrary and violent.'[16] The Levinasian critique of violence and its relation with morality is inherent here to the pre-political relationship of unique individuals, a relationship that precedes the institution of any totality. Levinas describes this encounter with the otherness of the Other as an awakening to the ethical. The encounter with the face (le visage) of the other individual and the intersubjective experience of the other person hints already to an ethical situation which transcends the tyranny of violence.

Taking violence seriously, as Levinas does, means taking the absolute otherness of the Other as an ethical event which transcends violence. Levinas' nonviolent appeal to the face of the other is more than simple private kindness and righteousness. His approach to responsibility as a selfless and non-reciprocal act is a true reminder of Gandhi's idea of suffering for the world and Martin Luther King's appropriation of the evangelical notion of Agape as a selfless love. For both Gandhi and King, facing the other at times of violence meant resuscitating and managing the humanity of humankind at crucial political crossroads. In the same manner, Levinas insists on the act of suffering for the Other as a form of taking responsibility for one's oppressor. Both Levinas and Gandhi insist on the process of substitution of the subject for the Other as a form of struggle for justice and an effort to elaborate a liberatory praxis. As Tahmasebi-Birgani points out adequately,

> The traces of Levinas' ethicopolitics can be seen in Gandhi's political rebellion and in his simultaneously nonviolent and revolutionary, patient and demanding, praxis. This notion of liberation has been made possible by holding on to an eschatological vision of peace whose laws of love and substitution resist disappearing into power politics. Gandhi's political praxis can help us understand the relevancy of Levinas' ethics of one-for-the-other for the radical politics of liberation – it is a praxis that keeps Levinas' ethics from being reduced to an individual virtue or collective charity and that enables us to see his ethicopolitics as the ground for a radical collective mobilization.[17]

Levinas' insistence on the otherness of the Other as a break with the centrality of power and an acknowledgement of the limits of violence and the possibility of nonviolence provides us with a satisfactory answer to the ethical essence of the political. If the question of the political is primarily a question of the relationship of the citizen-subject with a plurality of others-citizens, then this question immediately links the responsibility of the political to the limits of violence. As such, taking nonviolence as a serious alternative means taking the otherness of the Other as a waking call to our global responsibilities. Being for the Other and suffering for him/her is not possible within the horizons of the historic violence; it is only possible in the discontinuous time of nonviolent brotherhood and empathic friendship. As Robert L. Holmes explains,

> If nonviolence is thought of as a way of life, however, then as we have seen its end is not a far-off state of affairs but an ongoing process of infusing a certain quality into one's day-to-day engagement with the world. To live non-violently and to encourage others to do the same is the end, and the question is not whether nonviolence is effective (though one might ask whether it is effective in achieving other ends) but whether this or that person is successful at living non-violently. Here means and ends collapse into one another, because it is in part the particular means one adopts in pursuing the many short-range ends in life ('ends-in-view' as John Dewey called them) that go to make-up the end. Rather than being steps on a ladder to a lofty and remote destination, means on this view are more akin to ingredients in a recipe, the end or final product of which is made up of what is put into it.[18]

The ethicopolitical balance between the means and the end suggested by thinkers of nonviolence is the most important and the most difficult to achieve. Yet it turns our attention to the fact that despite any justification, violence is never legitimate. If that is really the case, then the problem of the limits of violence is situated somewhere between the divine-like institutions in the contemporary world and the eternal demonic aspect of human nature. What we can call 'the paradox of violence' is that the greatest evils in the world are performed by the greatest rationalities. Violence is committed by states and individuals not because they are devilish, but because they have a rational project of domination and governing the world and human beings. As Adorno points out majestically, 'Auschwitz begins wherever someone looks at a slaughterhouse and thinks they're only animals.'[19] The ethics of nonviolence deals not so much with what violence is, but with what violence has become. And just as peace is not only the end of war but also a different vision of the relation between the humans and the world, nonviolence is a reminder of the noblest and the most decent that survives in human beings under the greatest evil and the worst possible brutalities. In other words, dissent and disobedience are the first acts of nonviolence against the fallen view of humanity. Nonviolence starts when the individual regains his/her lost dignity. One needs to live rightly to put an end to the wrongs of life. This is how Henry David Thoreau understood civil disobedience and his own role as a dissenter. He opined that

> I think that we should be men first, and subjects afterward. It is not desirable to cultivate a respect for the law, so much as for the right. The only obligation which I have a right to assume, is to do at any

time what I think right. It is truly enough said, that a corporation has no conscience; but a corporation of conscientious men is a corporation with a conscience. Law never made men a whit more just; and, by means of their respect for it, even the well-disposed are daily made the agents of injustice.[20]

At the centre of Thoreau's analysis is the idea of a nonviolent and deliberate violation of a law is a Socratic manner of obeying one's conscience. Thoreau's attitude towards individual moral conscience and towards civil disobedience points very clearly and directly to the sociopolitical controversies of our own time. What would Thoreau say about the revolt of the students in Hong Kong and the civic protests in Chile, Iran, Lebanon and Algeria if he were alive today? He would have continued, undoubtedly, to refute the absolute legitimacy of governments and to be convinced that the moral law would prevail. Thoreau, like those who followed his path later, believed in the process of maturation and moral progress of humanity. What he wrote in 1847 was meditated and repeated by Albert Einstein in 1934 when he wrote about peace: 'May the conscience and the common sense of the peoples be awakened, so that we may reach a new stage in the life of nations, where people will look back on war as an incomprehensible aberration of their forefathers.'[21]

2

An Obligation to Dissent and to Disobey

Henry David Thoreau and After

The last two centuries have seen the growth of the modern state to the point where, in many nations of human civilization, it has come to be taken for granted as a natural course of political development of humanity for which we are destined, for better or for worse. Those who read and continue to analyze Henry David Thoreau's treatise *On the Duty of Civil Disobedience* will find themselves in an ambience very different from that which prevails in present-day discussions of civil disobedience. They will find there a deep and constant preoccupation of Thoreau with the ethical, a conception of the individual integrally related to fundamental moral and philosophical principles of nonviolence. Because Thoreau gave moral legitimacy to the obligation of the individual to disobey unjust laws, his critique of the state and his tendency towards individual dissent became an inspiration to many theorists and practitioners of nonviolence around the world, including Mahatma Gandhi and Martin Luther King, Jr.

Gandhi acknowledged his debt to Thoreau on many occasions, during his Satyagraha campaign in South Africa and later in his anti-colonial struggle in India. As Ramachandra Guha notes,

> In September 1907 the name of Henry David Thoreau appeared in the columns of Indian Opinion for the first time. Gandhi had only recently become acquainted with his tract on civil disobedience. The jail-going resolution of 11 September 1906 had been invented on the spot; in later weeks and months, Gandhi sought precedents in Indian traditions of boycott and protest. Then he began using the term 'passive resistance', whose origins lay rather in the boycott by Nonconformists of schools that indoctrinated their pupils in the teachings of the Church of England. Now a full year after the technique of protest was first proposed, the teachings of an American radical were invoked to support it. . . . But Gandhi also wrote that 'historians say that the chief cause of abolition of slavery in America was Thoreau's imprisonment and the publication by him of the above-mentioned book [On the Duty of Civil Disobedience] after his release.' No historians were named, perhaps because they could not be.[1]

Gandhi also acknowledged Thoreau in his preface to the English version of *Hind Swaraj* underlining that he has 'endeavoured humbly to follow Tolstoy, Ruskin, Thoreau, Emerson and other writers, besides the masters of Indian philosophy'.[2] Gandhi continued reading

Thoreau and being inspired by him throughout his nonviolent struggles for the independence of India.

> Gandhi did find in him ample confirmation for his new philosophy. . . . He was heartened to read that conscience, not majorities, should have the ultimate say in judging what is politically right or wrong, that while it is not one's duty to eradicate evil, it is certainly one's first duty not to give support to it, that even one person's action counts although the multitude may be opposed to it, that in an unjust political regime the prison is the right place for the just person, that only that state is worthy of obedience which recognizes the just individual 'as a higher and independent power' from which the state's own power is ultimately derived.[3]

Henry David Thoreau was also an important intellectual stimulation for the nonviolent resistance movement of Martin Luther King, Jr. in America. Writing about the Montgomery bus boycott, King affirms,

> As I thought further I came to see that what we were really doing was withdrawing our cooperation from an evil system, rather than merely withdrawing our economic support from the bus company. At this point I began to think about Thoreau's essay *On Civil Disobedience*. I remembered how, as a college student, I had been moved when I first read this work.[4]

King refers explicitly to Thoreau and his famous essay in different periods of his life and struggle and especially in his famous *Letter from Birmingham Jail* where Thoreau provides him with the moral justification for the act of lawbreaking. For King, as for Gandhi, it went without saying that in a nonviolent struggle disobeying unjust laws provided the powerless population with an extraordinary moral power. Henry David Thoreau was not a revolutionary and he did not consider civil disobedience as an act of revolution.

All that Thoreau wrote on civil disobedience more than 150 years ago reverberates forcefully in the nonviolent movements of the twenty-first century. According to Howard Zinn, 'Thoreau's essay propounded such a universal principle of human rights that it continues to be an inspiration for dissident thinkers and activists around the world.'[5] However, for a long period of time Thoreau was considered as an American transcendentalist who lived for some time at the Walden Pond and wrote anti-slavery essays such as 'Slavery in Massachusetts'. Strangely, when Thoreau published his essay 'Civil Disobedience' in Elizabeth Peabody's journal *Aesthetic Papers* in 1849, nobody would have guessed that more than half a century later it would be considered as a seminal work in political theory. There is an obvious similitude between Thoreau's defiance of the law in nineteenth-century America by choosing jail instead of payment of his poll-tax and the 2019 anti-government protests of the Chinese students in Hong Kong. Both Henry David Thoreau and the Hong Kong students knowingly broke the law but also strictly avoided any form of violence. Thoreau knew perfectly that since government depends on the obedience of the individual, the basic political assumption of nonviolent resistance lies in civil disobedience of the citizens. In ethical terms, Thoreauvian disobedience proved to be a case of conscience, the legitimization of a 'higher law' against the law of the King or that of the Republic and a response to the fear of the punishment. As such, Thoreau distinguished between political law and moral law, the latter representing the true dignity of the individual and humankind. He wrote in his famous essay 'Slavery in Massachusetts':

> Will mankind never learn that policy is not morality – that it never secures any moral right, but considers merely what is expedient? chooses the available candidate – who is invariably the Devil – and what right have his constituents to be surprised, because the Devil does not behave like an angel of light? What is wanted is men, not of policy, but of probity – who recognize a higher law than the Constitution, or the decision of the majority. The fate of the country does not depend on how you vote at the polls – the worst man is as strong as the best at that game; it does not depend on what kind of paper you drop into the ballot-box once a year, but on what kind of man you drop from your chamber into the street every morning.[6]

Thoreau did not believe in the normal channels of change, like the parliament in a republican regime. He, therefore, tried to change the public opinion on the issue of what is just and what is unjust. Thus, one of the novelties and originalities of Thoreauvian civil disobedience was to engage simultaneously both the government and the governed. However, in most of the nonviolent movements of the past seventy years the defiance of the regime and its illegitimacy has been one of the primary reasons for the rise of mass civil disobedience. In practically all the well-known cases of nonviolent resistance around the world, the choice to become civil disobedient was deliberately made as the regime or the laws of the land were considered illegitimate or/and unjust. Thoreau's own writings show his direct engagement with the concept of the law. Thoreau's concept of the law breathes the spirit of freedom – particularly when he echoed Marcus Tullius Cicero (106–43 BCE) that 'the law will never make men free; it is men who have got to make the law free'.[7] To a considerable extent Thoreau needed to define himself as against the law, not because he was an anarchist, but because as a transcendentalist and a reformer, he believed that the 'right to live' preceded the 'obligation to be governed'. As Len Gougeon points out correctly, in Thoreau, 'the perception of right is intuitive, a product of the heart rather than the head, which, in turn, is based upon the existence and efficacy of a "higher law" or the divinity in man'.[8] As such, Thoreau's attack on government is not an appeal to anarchy but an effort towards the moral progress of the citizens. Thoreau remained convinced that the moral progress of the citizens helped to reform and improve the government. Therefore, Thoreau believed that modern governments had failed miserably to help the citizens in having a life of virtue and excellence. For Thoreau, governments were only interested in the bodies of the citizens, without taking into account their consciences. 'The mass of men serve the State thus', affirms Thoreau,

> not as men mainly, but as machines, with their bodies. They are the standing army, and the militia, jailers, constables, *posse comitatus*, &c. In most cases there is no free exercise whatever of the judgment or of the moral sense; but they put themselves on a level with wood and earth and stones; and wooden men can perhaps be manufactured that will serve the purpose as well. Such command no more respect than men of straw or a lump of dirt. They have the same sort of worth only as horses and dogs. Yet such as these even are commonly esteemed good citizens. Others,

– as most legislators, politicians, lawyers, ministers, and office-holders, – serve the state chiefly with their heads; and, as they rarely make any moral distinctions, they are as likely to serve the Devil, without intending it, as God. A very few, as heroes, patriots, martyrs, reformers in the great sense, and men, serve the state with their consciences also, and so necessarily resist it for the most part; and they are commonly treated as enemies by it.[9]

Such indications of the negative role of the state and the frailty of the life of citizens is accentuated by Thoreau at the end of his book *Life without Principle*, where he digresses from what he calls the 'dyspepsia' of the states and individuals. As he emphasizes,

A man may become conscious of some of the processes of digestion in a morbid state, and so have the dyspepsia, as it is called. It is as if a thinker submitted himself to be rasped by the great gizzard of creation. Politics is, as it were, the great gizzard of society, full of grit and gravel, and the two political parties are its two opposing halves – sometimes split into quarters, it may be, which grind each other. Not only individuals, but States, have thus a confirmed dyspepsia, which expresses itself, you can imagine by what sort of eloquence. Thus our life is not altogether a forgetting, but also, alas! to a great extent, a remembering of that which we should never have been conscious of, certainly not in our waking hours.[10]

In the eyes of Henry David Thoreau, American politics as a whole appears to be dyspeptic.

Having established the dyspeptic nature of the state, Thoreau endorses the exercise of an active conscience as a transcendental self-culture for the individual. He specifically calls upon Truth, that according to him, is 'always in harmony with herself, and is not concerned chiefly to reveal the justice that may consist with wrong-doing'.[11] Ralph Waldo Emerson called Thoreau 'a speaker and actor of the truth . . . [whose] soul was made for the noblest society'.[12] Indeed, Thoreau's writings reveal a nobility of spirit and a quest for truth which develop an ethics of nonviolence directed towards a non-utilitarian view of the world. As his readers know, Thoreau never championed one spiritual tradition over another. He was a true philosopher of the East and the West.

> In contrast to Emerson, who used his Asian readings mostly to illustrate or dramatize his own ideas, Thoreau found them indispensible in the formation of his own personalized spirituality. He looked to the Vedas, as well as to Pythagoras, to make sense of his spiritual delight in music; he looked to Manu to support his personal notions of bodily asceticism and literary organicism; and he looked to the Gita to clarify the nature of his own spontaneous episodes of ecstatic experience, as well as the importance of devotion and disinterested action in pursuing his own literary work.[13]

However, though Thoreau represented a romantic figure to many of his contemporaries and his future readers and followers, he also remained a heroic representative of nonviolent democratic dissent. Thoreau continues to confront us as a dissenter, with his civic obligation to disobey. As such, Thoreau's contribution to the philosophy of nonviolent resistance is exemplified by lawless individuality which engaged him critically with the American society of his time. Thoreau's admiration for Captain John Brown's radical struggle against slavery was the most indisputable and unmistakable expression of his nonviolent dissent and democratic disobedience. In his essay *A Plea for Captain John Brown*, Thoreau described John Brown and his disobedience in these terms:

> No man has appeared in America as yet who loved his fellow man so well, and treated him so tenderly. He lived for him. He took up his life and he laid it down for him. . . . It seems as if no man had ever died in America before, or in order to die you must first have lived. . . . These men, in teaching us how to die, have at the same time taught us how to live.[14]

Thoreau's insistence on the art of dying, as much as on the art of living, is a principal part of his philosophy of nonviolent dissent, as is the case for most of the practitioners of nonviolence. Thoreau did not consider life as an 'idle amusement'.[15] Quite the contrary; standing in life for Thoreau was much more than just having an opinion of it. For Thoreau, the purpose of life's journey, as explored in *Walden*, is to seek and scrutinize the moral and spiritual potentials of nature as a point of departure for a quest of Truth. The mind-boggling evidence in *Walden* is that 'living becomes a matter of self-culture, because – as [Thoreau] discovered during his night in jail (which occurred while he was living at the pond) – one's neighbors can seldom be coaxed into exploring new views. Life with principle can be a lonely journey'.[16] Thoreau reminds us in *Walden* that his lifelong journey is nothing but what Gandhi would call seventy years later 'My Experiments with Truth'. From one point of view, *Walden* is the philosophical foundation of *Civil Disobedience*. The point here is not too much to present Thoreau as an inward explorer as to demonstrate that Thoreau was essentially a gadfly dropping out of mainstream culture because of his non-conformity and his principle of passive resistance. This is why and how Thoreau became a universal name in an ever-widening circle. The reason is simple: Thoreau's dissentient nonviolence was more attractive to a partisan age like the twentieth century. It is certainly more difficult for a conformist and populist age like ours.

Henry David Thoreau praised a confrontational form of nonviolent resistance. 'From the mid-1840s forward, then, the hero in Thoreau's major writings is the aggressive, confrontational individual who "fronts" the democratic state and just about everything else.'[17] It is widely agreed that if Thoreau advocated an experimental mode of approach, rather than a cognitive method, to life and truth, it is because he believed that it made 'the laws of the universe' more accessible. It was left to Thoreau to work these laws in relation to his political philosophy of engaged individualism and law of conscience. We find this political philosophy in *Civil Disobedience*. As Walter Harding points out,

> Its fundamental principle is the Transcendentalist one that that there is a higher law than civil law – the law of conscience – and that when these laws are in conflict, it is the citizen's duty to obey the voice of God within rather than that of civil authority without. If he will go to prison rather than obey an evil law, he will through his courage and martyrdom arouse the conscience of his people to rebel *en masse* and though their resistance they will clog the machinery of tyranny by filling the courts and the jails and thus bring about repeal of the offensive law.[18]

Of course, it goes without saying that in Thoreau, unlike in Gandhi and King, there is no reference to mass civil disobedience. However, Thoreau makes reference to the Socratic principle of self-examination and the right of the individual to do what he/she thinks is right. Thoreau clearly articulates this moral right when he writes:

> I think that we should be men first, and subjects afterward. It is not desirable to cultivate a respect for the law, so much as for the right. The only obligation which I have a right to assume is to do at any time what I think right. It is truly enough said that a corporation has no conscience; but a corporation of conscientious men is a corporation with a conscience. Law never made men a whit more just; and, by means of their respect for it, even the well-disposed are daily made the agents of injustice.[19]

Thoreau knows well that his reference to the individual moral conscience is right. He knows that even if he is a minority of one, the truth is the truth. According to him, an honest individual who is fighting for justice has to confront heroically the unjust laws. 'Unjust laws exist', says Thoreau, but

> shall we be content to obey them, or shall we endeavor to amend them, and obey them until we have succeeded, or shall we transgress them at once? Men generally, under such a government as this, think that they ought to wait until they have persuaded the majority to alter them. They think that, if they should resist, the remedy would be worse than the evil. But it is the fault of the government itself that the remedy is worse than the evil. It makes it

worse. Why is it not more apt to anticipate and provide for reform? Why does it not cherish its wise minority? Why does it cry and resist before it is hurt? Why does it not encourage its citizens to be on the alert to point out its faults, and do better than it would have them? Why does it always crucify Christ, and excommunicate Copernicus and Luther, and pronounce Washington and Franklin rebels?[20]

At this level of nonviolent resistance against the evil, Thoreau shifts from the concept of an inward self-transformation based on the Socratic idea of listening to one's inner voice to the transformation of the society at large. As a matter of fact, the Thoreauvian individual quest for justice turns into a civil disobedience of the law. Thoreau's ethico-political disobedience is, therefore, neither a blind subjection, nor an anarchistic rejection of negative liberty. Actually, in the manner of Antigone, it reaches out to a higher principle beyond the laws of the *polis* (city state). In Sophocles' powerful play, *Antigone*, the daughter of Oedipus defies the edict of King Creon of Thebes that her brother's corpse should be left on the streets for birds and vultures to feast on. When Creon charges her with disobedience of the law, Antigone replies:

Of course I did. It wasn't Zeus, not in the least, who made this proclamation, not to me. Nor did that Justice, dwelling with the gods beneath the earth, ordain such laws for men. Nor did I think your edict had such force that you, a mere mortal, could override the gods, the great unwritten, unshakable traditions. They are alive, not just today or yesterday: they live forever from the first of time, and no one knows when they first saw the light.[21]

This act of disobedience, which ultimately costs Antigone her life, is a reflection on the limits of the legitimacy of the laws and the state. All through history, we have seen many symbolic Antigones, Thoreau included, who have been involved in such an act of disobedience, by daring to think by themselves and speaking back to power. Thoreau's essay *On Civil Disobedience* is a great reminder of Antigone's perennial moral courage and heroic status.

Today's readers of Sophocles' *Antigone* or Thoreau's *On Civil Disobedience* and the practitioners of nonviolence against tyrannies or illiberal electoral democracies do certainly sympathize with both. This raises the essential question of the moral and political choice between a society which aspires to justice and fairness and one which fails to be just and fair. Citizens without the choice of their political future and a say on the laws are lesser human beings lost on a road with no billboards. Healthy democracies need vibrant public spaces and citizens like Henry David Thoreau and Antigone who can operate in the daylight and with transparency. Excluding the views of nonviolent individuals in the name of sedition and rebellion is not only absurd, it is also politically immature. The problem with a majoritarian democracy is that it is not designed to find solutions for complex problems. A government with a majority which appeals to the nationalistic sentiments of the voters can become as authoritarian as a dictatorial one. But democracy is not about populism or nationalism. Democracy is about the right of minorities (ethnic, religious, sexual, intellectual etc.) and the art of celebrating diversity. In continuity of Antigone's moral courage and individual heroism, Thoreau asked his contemporaries and future generations to stand witness for nonviolence and peace, while objecting to the unjust laws of the state. 'One thing about Thoreau keeps him very near to me,' Walt Whitman affirmed. 'I refer to his lawlessness – his dissent – his going his absolute own road let hell blaze all it chooses.'[22] Thoreau's philosophy taught individuals like Mohandas Karamchand Gandhi and Martin Luther King, Jr. not only the way to practise the art of dissent, but also how to handle political struggle. More importantly, like Antigone, he left us with a powerful appeal to a harmony between the laws of humankind and higher laws. Thoreau's belief in higher laws and defiant individualism opened the path to Gandhian nonviolent resistance in the twentieth century. Thoreau, Gandhi, King, Mandela and Havel were all individuals who acted on the imperatives of their moral consciences. The truth is that Thoreau's central concern, stated in all his writings, but mainly in his essay *On Civil Disobedience*, is the 'thick action' of the citizens which is needed to fulfil democratic existence. But to speak like Martin Luther King, Jr., how can we talk about the democratization of democracies if there is no 'publicness' of action and free speech of citizens? Thoreau was well aware of this. The 'political' that Thoreau seeks to revive is a space of democratic coexistence which transcends the 'thin paper' of the American constitution. Its core is autonomy, not simply as independence from outside forces, but an autonomy enabled by the individual *conatus* for democracy, and also by the citizen's capacity to make beginnings in politics and to express autonomy and freedom in action. It is the citizen's capacity to act, to speak and to create shared spaces through interaction with others, as it is defined and dictated by the ethical imperative of civic friendship and nonviolent resistance. If there is only one thing that the Thoreauvian experience of civil disobedience shows us, it is that citizens need an experience of moral conscience, since many of them seem to have forgotten that democratic governance is not a power over the society, but a power within it. In other words, if democracy equals self-rule and self-control of the citizens, empowerment of the civil society and the collective ability to rule democratically are the essential constituents of democratic governance. Democracy and nonviolence, therefore, are inseparable. Where democracy is practised, the rules of the political game are defined by the absence of violence. If democracy were no more than a set of institutional guarantees, how could citizens be capable of thinking politics today and struggle for the emergence of new perspectives of democratic action? And how are we to reconcile the twin convictions that there can be no democracy unless state-centred power is limited and that there can be no democracy without the pursuit of nonviolence? Mankind cannot escape politics without abdicating its humanity as a political animal. But politics is not only the conquest and the preservation of power; it is mainly, as the ancient Greek philosophers thought, the embodiment of the ethical in a historical community. So not all politics is corrupt per se, and not all political powers are evil. But once established, the politics which is conceived in violence necessitates violent action to sustain its own existence. That is to say, there is a paradox between the constitution of the political as an art of governing and the reality of violence.

So what does the Thoreauvian moral obligation to disobey unjust laws show us? First and foremost, that nonviolent disobedience as a mode of thinking and acting or as a way of living contributes to the spiritual rebirth of the citizen (who lives in a democracy or is under tyranny) and helps to renew the question of the otherness of the Other. In other words, Thoreau never ceased to assert that human beings should live with their moral conscience and listen to their inner voice, while having love and compassion for other living beings. Thoreau's transcendentalist individualism was based on the assumption that human beings are moral animals and therefore no action should be taken by the individual at the expense of the freedom and welfare of others. As such, Thoreau helps us to review what we consider as everyday reality, simply by contrasting the life in which we everyday sale to the virtuous life that he would have citizens lead. The political implications of Thoreau's philosophy of life end up with an existential struggle between moral laws and the laws of the state. As Thoreau believes, justice and honesty are moral gains. Therefore, it is worth fighting for them. That is why he calls greatest gains 'the highest reality'. This is the emphasis at the heart of his masterpiece *Walden*. 'The greatest gains and values are farthest from being appreciated. We easily come to doubt if they exist. We soon forget them. They are the highest reality.'[23] Gandhi considered Truth as the highest spiritual reality. He, too, believed that the fate of humanity is in being truthful and speaking back to injustice. One might say that both Thoreau and Gandhi made their life's work to introduce disobedience into our moral syntax. This was certainly because they believed that life is not about hedonistic living, but to serve others. Gandhi's experiments with truth gave him the courage to follow the path of Thoreau in order to find that

> Submission to the State law is the price a citizen pays for his personal liberty. Submission, therefore, to a State law wholly or largely unjust is an immoral barter for liberty. A citizen who thus realizes the evil nature of a State is not satisfied to live on its

sufferance, and therefore appears to the others who do not share his belief to be a nuisance to society whilst he is endeavoring to compel the State, without committing a moral breach, to arrest him. Thus considered, civil resistance is a most powerful expression of a soul's anguish and an eloquent protest against the continuance of an evil State.[24]

The history of nonviolent resistance entered a new phase with the life and struggles of Mahatma Gandhi. Though Gandhi humbly dismissed all through his life what might be called by the name of 'Gandhism', there is no doubt that the world continues to feel and live the effects of his philosophy of nonviolence. That is to say, there is no Gandhian philosophy more important than nonviolence and there never will be; on the contrary, Gandhian philosophy is more important for nonviolence than ever before.

3

Bringing Ethics into Politics

The Gandhian Satyagraha

As early as 1909, in his seminal work *Hind Swaraj*, Gandhi had identified 'nonviolence' as a key concept of his ethical living. Gandhi was concerned with teaching his fellow Indians that modern civilization was a factory civilization which produced violence. Years later, in October 1939, he told the members of the executive board of Gandhi Seva Sangh, 'I would ask you to read *Hind Swaraj* with my eyes and see therein the chapter on how to make India nonviolent. You cannot build nonviolence on a factory civilization, but it can be built on self-contained villages.'[1] Gandhi believed that through *Hind Swaraj*, followed by his campaigns of passive resistance in South Africa, he would be able to introduce Indians to a new conception of *ahimsa* that would help them to overcome the materialistic and utilitarian essence of the modern world. Through his South African campaigns, Gandhi was brought to reflect on the nature of *ahimsa* as it was discussed and practised by Hinduism, Jainism and Buddhism. Yet, though Gandhi claimed to be a Hindu, his practice of *ahimsa* was more experimental than theological and he never based his nonviolence on an organized religion or any other fixed ideal. As he mentioned all through his life, nonviolence was part of his continuing quest for Truth. He wrote in July 1926, 'Non-violence is the greatest force man has been endowed with. Truth is the only goal he has. For God is none other than Truth. But Truth cannot be, never will be, reached except through nonviolence.'[2] With Truth as the goal of nonviolent action, Gandhi refused to separate spirituality and politics. Yet, unlike many of the Indian gurus and saints, Gandhi was not a practising mystic, nor was he a typical party politician like Tilak, Gokhale, or even Nehru. Also, despite his close encounters with the Indian masses, Gandhi's method of nonviolent struggle remained very critical of the mobs. As a result, the virtue and the meaning of nonviolence were conferred by Gandhi to a doctrine that he formulated out of his resistance in South Africa.

Consequently, for Gandhi, nonviolence signified not only not bringing harm to others, but also accepting voluntary self-suffering in order to transform a situation from confrontational to compassionate and persuasive. For Gandhi, then, the courage to practise nonviolence meant the moral preparation and readiness to respect and empathize with the otherness of the Other. As Gandhi repeated often, nonviolence was not passive but active courage. Not happy to see his movement being called by the English phrase 'Passive Resistance', Gandhi decided to go for a more appropriate term for his movement. 'In 1907 Indian Opinion announced a small prize for an alternative, which Maganlal won with his suggestion of "sadagraha" or "firmness for the good". Gandhi altered the prize-winning entry to "Satyagraha" or "firmness for the truth".'[3] Gandhian *Satyagraha* was distinct from all the previous methods of armed struggle against colonization. 'The distinctiveness of Gandhi's method lay in shaming the rulers by voluntary suffering, with resisters seeking beatings and imprisonment by breaking laws in a nonviolent yet utterly determined manner.'[4] Obviously, Gandhi found proofs of the power of his Satyagraha in Thoreau's *Civil Disobedience*. However, as we can see in *Hind Swaraj* and Gandhi's own *Autobiography*, Gandhi's celebration of Satyagraha went hand in hand with his severe condemnation of Western civilization. This critique was also based on his reading of other Western writers like Leo Tolstoy and John Ruskin. Tolstoy's Christian philosophy, especially, was a revelation to Gandhi. In an obituary written after Tolstoy's death in November 1910, Gandhi wrote: 'He [Tolstoy] was for us more than one of the greatest men of his age. We have endeavored, as far as possible, and as far as we understood it, to follow his teaching.'[5] Certainly, Gandhi did not follow all that Tolstoy preached, but he found a strong argument for his own nonviolence in Tolstoy's idea of 'non-resistance to evil'. Praising Tolstoy, Gandhi appropriated this idea for the Indian context while fortifying his own theory of nonviolence. He noted:

> When a man like Tolstoy, one of the clearest thinkers in the western world, one of the greatest writers, one who as a soldier has known what violence is and what it can do, condemns Japan for having blindly followed the law of modern science, falsely so-called, and fears for that country 'the greatest calamities', it is for us to pause and consider whether, in our impatience of English rule, we do not want to replace one evil by another and a worse . . . . If we do not want the English in India we must pay the price. Tolstoy indicates it. 'Do not resist evil, but also do not yourselves participate in evil

– in the violent deeds of the administration of the law courts, the collection of taxes and, what is more important, of the soldiers, and no one in the world will enslave you,' passionately declares the sage of Yasnaya Polyana.[6]

It goes without saying that with his readings of Tolstoy and Thoreau, Gandhi's scope of nonviolence was exceptionally expanded. He clearly distanced himself from the traditional conception of ahimsa in Hinduism, which he described as a 'cloistered virtue'. He affirmed, 'Non-violence is not a cloistered virtue to be practised by the individual for his peace and final salvation, but a rule of conduct for society if it is to live consistently with human dignity.'[7] By saying this, Gandhi was differentiating between his experiences in nonviolence and the ahimsa of the Indian rishis and saints. In the words of Gandhi himself, nonviolence was an 'active love' rather than a 'passive spirituality'. According to Bhikhu Parekh, Gandhi agreed that India

had made great discoveries in the past in the sphere of nonviolence, but insisted that these were inadequate and needed to be supplemented by the insights of other religions. In effect, he told his countrymen that, contrary to their frequent claims, they not only had no monopoly of the understanding of nonviolence but also that their view of it was partial and limited. Gandhi thought it was his historic task to integrate the profoundest insights of the Indian and non-Indian traditions of nonviolence and to develop a more satisfactory view of it.[8]

Though Gandhi's critical detachment from the unworldly meaning of nonviolence provoked a great deal of protest, it also opened new perspectives for the modern philosophy of nonviolence and a radical redefinition of the concept of otherness of the Other. For Gandhi this effort of redefinition of nonviolence resided in two elements: on the one hand, replacing the concept of self-interest by that of self-respect and self-restraint. Human beings needed to be dignified in order to have the capacity to organize a plural polity. On the other hand, human interdependence and solidarity were born out of ethical experiments with Truth. As such, for Gandhi, the *condition sine qua non* of a harmonious sociopolitical life was the moral and spiritual development of the individuals. As a result,

> the state should become not a collection of isolated individuals with nothing to unite them save their abstract citizenship, but a community of communities, a loosely structured federation of lively and organic social units. . . . Self-governing local communities and associations could take over many of the functions . . . monopolized by the government and, thus, increasingly reduce the role of law and coercion.[9]

Gandhi knew that his experiments in democratic decentralization in particular and ethicalization of politics in general involved a radical inversion of modern political theory. However, he insisted on being the agent of this rupture himself by suggesting the empowerment of the self-governing communities against the highly centralized modern state. Gandhi considered the modern state as a source of violence, because it 'did not activate the moral energies of its citizens. [And] it was impersonal and bureaucratic, a "soulless machine" which ruled by means of rigid rules and discouraged personal responsibility and initiative. It made a fetish of territorial integrity, thought little of sacrificing human lives in defending every inch of it and jealously demanded its citizens' exclusive loyalty.[10] Therefore, according to Gandhi, the crisis of modern civilization was moral in nature and no nonviolent resistance was possible unless it was moral and spiritual in nature. But Gandhi differed from other revolutionaries and his nonviolent revolution in the twentieth century differed from that of all Third World anti-imperialists and anti-colonialists. Gandhi refused to accept political power and this attitude

> was linked with his refusal to devise more than a tentative programme for the society that might emerge from a nonviolent revolution. In accepting the power to direct others he would be depriving them from the right to conduct their own 'experiments with truth', and in devising a rigid social structure for the future he would be denying the mutability of the quest for Truth.[11]

Gandhi's vision of nonviolence was strikingly realistic and pragmatic. What interested him in combining ethics and politics was not the lust for power, but the spiritual implications of a political action. 'Gandhi was one of the most able politicians of his time, and all the more remarkable because, remembering the lessons of the *Bhagavad Gita*, he never sought for the rewards of politics. . . . So he became the destroyer of an empire, and in the process felt that he was doing nothing contrary to his *dharma*, his religious duty.'[12] Unlike many of his contemporaries who considered religion as a theo-ontological construction and subjected the realm of the political to the laws of God, Gandhi considered religion as a vehicle for universal ethics and a collective wisdom which was passed on from one generation to the next. However, Gandhi endorsed a secular state that did not deny spiritual transcendence of the citizens, but he abhorred all forms of religious nationalism. He indisputably rejected the idea of India as a Hindu nation, though, as it was pointed previously, he founded many elements of his theory of nonviolence in the spiritual tradition of Hinduism. As such, he saw an unequivocal relationship between the process of nonviolent resistance and religious pluralism. As he affirmed in *Hind Swaraj*:

> India cannot cease to be one nation because people belonging to different religions live in it. The introduction of foreigners does not necessarily destroy the nation; they merge in it. A country is one nation only when such a condition obtains in it. That country must have a faculty for assimilation. India has ever been such a country. In reality there are as many religions as there are individuals; but those who are conscious of the spirit of nationality do not interfere with one another's religion. If they do, they are not fit to be considered a nation. If the Hindus believe that India should be peopled only by Hindus, they are living in dream-land. The Hindus, the Mahomedans, the Parsis and the Christians who have made India their country are fellow-countrymen, and they will have to live in unity, if only for their own interest. In no part of the world are one nationality and one religion synonymous terms; nor has it ever been so in India.[13]

Gandhi's philosophy of nonviolence was also reinforced by his theory of civic and empathic republicanism. His belief in nonviolence as *Satyagraha* (firmness for the truth), *Swaraj* (self-rule) and *Sarvodaya* (welfare of all) was supported by his notion of community as a pluralistic political entity. Gandhi, more than anybody else, understood the impossibility of an absolute nonviolent state. However, he believed that the role of a minimal non-coercive state and dutiful and responsible citizens would be to establish a social order free of violence. Briefly, Gandhi had a clear picture of the nonviolent society as a public space where politics and moral virtue work together. As Anthony Parel points out rightly, 'It is implicit in Gandhi's political philosophy that civic virtues without the cooperation of the state cannot create a nonviolent social order. . . . If the policies of a state do not reflect the values of his system of virtues, the social order could hardly become nonviolent.'[14] As a result, in a Gandhian society both the state and the citizens should be virtuous, since the political balance rests on their mutual understanding about the inherent dignity of the Other. In other words, Gandhi ties nonviolence to respect for the otherness of the Other. As such, Gandhi believes that at the level of citizenship, by and large, the ethics of responsibility is more significant than the ethics of conviction. For this reason, he argues that every citizen is responsible for the other, especially in a situation of corruption and lawlessness of the state. Disobeying the laws of an evil and corrupt state is, therefore, the duty of each citizen. Going further, Gandhi claimed:

Most people do not understand the complicated machinery of the government. They do not realize every citizen silently but none the less certainly sustains the government of the day in ways of which he has no knowledge. Every citizen therefore renders himself responsible for every act of his government. And it is quite proper to support it so long as the actions of the government are bearable. But when they hurt him and his nation it becomes his duty to withdraw his support.[15]

This is where Gandhi's ethico-spiritual Satyagraha and Thoreau's transcendentalist civil disobedience join hands. He initiates a process of non-cooperation and disobedience that aims at revealing the unjust nature of power. Gandhi, however, is also well conscious about the power of nonviolence as a proactive and not only a reactive element. As Ronald Terchek asserts, 'Moving beyond conventional views of power, Gandhi offers an expansive and intensive understanding of power. He sees it residing in places and practices ignored, or even denied, by most observers. . . . Gandhi plows further, taking an unexpected direction. For him, love is also a form of power.'[16]

Gandhi makes love one of the key elements of his nonviolence. According to him, love is the foundation of all interconnectedness and dialogue. It is, thus, an ability to take into consideration the otherness of the Other. 'Non-violence means an ocean of compassion,'[17] wrote Gandhi. For Gandhi, nonviolence meant promoting the livelihood of all living beings, while refraining from selfishness and humiliating others. Moreover, in relation to the otherness of the Other, Gandhi developed his nonviolence as a dual approach to the problem of suffering: on the one hand, suffering for others, and on the other hand, relieving others from their sufferings. Going back to Tolstoy's law of love as the core philosophy of Christian ethics, Gandhi formulated his notion of 'Sarvodaya' as the third important pillar of his philosophy of nonviolence, next to Satyagraha and Swaraj. Inspired by Ruskin's Unto This Last (which he read in South Africa), Gandhi prepared a paraphrased version of the book in Gujarati under the title Sarvodaya (the welfare of all) which he used in opposition against the utilitarian notion of 'the greatest good of the greatest number'. Many years later, in 1926, Gandhi contrasted the concept of self-sacrifice, as an important component of his nonviolent resistance, with this utilitarian concept. He wrote: 'A votary of *ahimsa* cannot subscribe to the utilitarian formula. He will strive for the greatest good of all and die in the attempt to realize the ideal. He will, therefore, be willing to die so that the others may live. He will serve himself with the rest by himself dying.'[18] Gandhi firmly held the community life of labour and sharing as part of his ideal of a nonviolent society. As a matter of fact, Gandhi also held that moral resistance against an evil state and its institutions should be accompanied by the idea of a harmonious society. Gandhi called on the modern citizens of the Indian society and the world to exercise their citizenship in terms of rights and duties by promoting justice and nonviolence. As Parel affirms,

> Very typically, the spiritual life for Gandhi was inseparable from action in the world, from the active life in the fields of politics, economics, and social reform. In this respect his spirituality differed radically from the spirituality of the yogis and ascetics of the past and the present. Social and political action informed by true spirituality was able to take the true measure of wealth, power and pleasure.[19]

In simple terms, for Gandhi, the welfare of one's soul and the welfare of the other were complementary. In this sense, the Gandhian exercise of citizenship in terms of autonomy (Swaraj) but also in relation to the two notions of duty and interconnectedness (Sarvodaya) is actually the coming together of moral resistance with social and economic reforms of civil society and the spiritualization of political life. Fundamentally, anyone who approaches the Gandhian philosophy will be struck by the variety of concepts and themes that are in play in the making of the concept of nonviolence.

Let us not forget that Gandhi made his ashrams, both in South Africa and in India, models of fanatic-free and caste-free society. India being a multilingual, multi-ethnic and multi-religious society, Gandhi was more concerned than Henry David Thoreau about the problems of communal harmony and interfaith dialogue. In this context it is useful to recall that for Gandhi the nonviolent struggle for the independence of India was expressed in terms of civic nationalism and not necessarily 'Hindu Raj' or casteism. In Gandhi's view, Indian betterment thus lay in the realm of ethical civism rather than in the working of a mythical religious government. Also, the civic and dialogical quality of Gandhi's nonviolence allowed him to go beyond all forms of narrow and egocentric self-interest, which failed to have a compassionate and empathic opinion of the enemy. He observed:

> I myself have always believed in the honesty of my enemies, and if one believes in it hard enough, one finds it. My enemies took advantage of my trust in them and deceived me. They deceived me eleven times running; and with stupid obstinacy, I went on believing in their honesty. With the result that, the twelfth time, they couldn't help keeping their word. Discovering their own honesty was a happy surprise for them and for me too. That is why my enemies and I have always parted very pleased with each other.[20]

From Gandhi's quote, we can conclude that Gandhi considered the practice of nonviolence not only along the Thoreauvian line of individual dissent and disobedience, but also as a civic dialogue which included the force of the soul. As shown in *Hind Swaraj* and his other writings, Gandhi's aim was to persuade the British colonialists of the wrongness of their cause, while voicing a new Indian nationalism in terms of empathic dialogue and communal harmony. Gandhi believed that it was vital to empower the powerless men and women by giving a considerable degree of self-determination to villages and communities. This is what Gandhi called by the name of 'Constructive Programme'. Gandhi defined Constructive Programme as a series of nonviolent processes to improve the structures of a community. Interestingly, Gandhi considered Constructive Programme as a more effective tool in the struggle for nonviolence than individual dissent or mass disobedience. He spelt this out in *Harijan* in 1940:

> Many Congressmen are playing at nonviolence. They think in terms of civil disobedience anyhow, meaning the filling of jails. This is a childish interpretation of the great force that civil disobedience is. I must continue to repeat, even though it may cause nausea, that prison-going without the backing of honest constructive effort and goodwill in the heart for the wrong-doer is violence and therefore forbidden in Satyagraha. . . . The constructive work prescribed by the Congress is the proper training. Those, therefore, who wish to see India realize her destiny through nonviolence should devote every ounce of their energy towards the fulfilment of the constructive programme in right earnest without any thought of civil disobedience.[21]

Gandhi was conscious about limiting disobedience against the government and unjust laws. Understanding this, Gandhi was not troubled by the idea of self-suffering or fasting unto death. Actually, in the Gandhian philosophy or resistance, we can find the intertwining of nonviolence and exemplary suffering. Perhaps self-sacrifice is the closest we come to ethical dying, in the sense that it is a principled leave-taking from life, an abandonment of one's petty preoccupations in order to see things more clearly. As such, there is a process of learning in the Gandhian act of self-suffering. For Socrates, to philosophize was to learn how to die. In the same way, for Gandhi, the practice of nonviolence starts with an act of self-sacrifice and the courage of dying for truth. Socrates inspired Gandhi by the importance of self-sacrifice and the art of dying at a time when the latter was developing his idea of Satyagraha in South Africa. Gandhi referred to Socrates as a 'Soldier of Truth' (*satyavir*) who had the willingness to fight unto death for his cause. His portrayal of Socrates as a Satyagrahi and a moral hero went hand in hand with the affirmation of the courage and audacity of a nonviolent warrior in the face of life-threatening danger. Consequently, for Gandhi, there was a close link between the use of nonviolence and the art of dying, in the same manner that cowardice was closely related to the practice of violence. According to Gandhi, 'Just as one must learn the art of killing in the training for violence, so one must learn the art of dying in the training for nonviolence.'[22]

Gandhi remained a believer in the art of self-sacrifice all his life. Though not a philosopher, Gandhi admired moral and political philosophers, who, in the manner of Socrates, were ready to struggle and die for the Truth. Like Socrates, Gandhi was neither a mystic nor a hermit. He was a civic actor and a practitioner of dissident citizenship. Gandhi considered Socrates' civic action as a source of virtue and moral strength. He affirmed: 'We pray to God, and want our readers also to pray, that they, and we too, may have the moral strength which enabled Socrates to follow virtue to the end and to embrace death as if it were his beloved. We advise everyone to turn his mind again and again to Socrates' words and conduct.'[23]

Gandhi's approach to death exemplified another Socratic aspect: courage. Gandhi believed that when fighting injustice, the actor must not only have the courage of his or her opinions but also be ready to give his or her life for the cause. As George Woodcock says, 'the idea of perishing for a cause, for other men, for a village even, occurs more frequently in Gandhi's writings as time goes on. He had always held that *satyagraha* implied the willingness to accept not only suffering but also death for the sake of a principle.'[24] Gandhi's dedication to justice in the face of death was an example of his courageous attitude of mind as a nonviolent resister. Further, one can find in Gandhi a readiness to raise the matter of dying as public policy. This is a state of mind which we can find as the background motto of Gandhi's political and intellectual life. Indeed, for Gandhi, the art of dying is very often a public act and an act of publicizing one's will to be free. There is something revealing in the parallel that Gandhi established between the struggle for freedom and the art of dying. In a speech at a meeting of the Congress in Bombay at the beginning of August 1942, he invited his fellow freedom fighters to follow a new *mantra*:

> Here is a *mantra*, a short one, that I give to you. You may imprint it on your hearts and let every breath of yours give expression to it. The *mantra* is 'Do or Die.' We shall either free India or die in the attempt; we shall not live to see the perpetuation of our slavery. Every true Congressman or woman will join the struggle with inflexible determination not to remain alive to see the country in bondage and slavery. . . . He who loses his life will gain it, he who

will seek to save it shall lose it. Freedom is not for the coward or the faint-hearted.[25]

Gandhi's ethical politics was strikingly evident in his empathic capacity towards others and in his being capable of seeing things as they did. This was a strategic knowledge that fostered nonviolence and sought to chart a course away from the violence of modernity. As such, the Gandhian effort of nonviolence could, to this day, be considered as an ability to rethink the human civilization in terms of a process of emancipatory questioning. Gandhian nonviolence was exemplary, not because Gandhi possessed any special Truth from which others were excluded, but because he remained always ready to comprehend and take into account the experiments of others with Truth. Consequently, unlike Thoreau's individualized disobedience, Gandhi's practice of nonviolence democratized dissent. The moral integrity of Gandhi made him a wise dissenter par excellence. His examined life was an end in itself, but more as a way to put into question the truths and beliefs that were at the foundation of communal life. As a dissident mind, Gandhi brought about a revaluation of the values of his time. As a critical mind and a practitioner of nonviolence, Gandhi was a committed gadfly, who was available to the others and engaged in a dialogue with them, because he was aware of the fact that dialogue defeats fanaticism, dogmatism and violence. Gandhi appears to many around the world today as a spiritual man who tried to find a harmonious balance between a contemplative life and a life of action, but, actually, both as a thinker and a practitioner of nonviolence, he was a disobedient mind who stood up against all forms of injustice. As a principled nonviolent resister, he adhered to nonviolence by conviction and not out of expediency. But this conviction was not temporal. On the contrary, Gandhi considered it as being universal and eternal. Because of this Gandhi saw nonviolence as a possibility for a better world. Nonviolence could be pursued at any moment of history and in any culture. As long as human civilization is alive, Gandhian nonviolence is an open door for all those powerless men, women and children who seek social, economic and political power. This is how we can evaluate the broader contribution of Gandhi to nonviolent protest movements around the world. That is why for seven decades Gandhi has been an inspiration for several generations of nonviolent freedom fighters in the West and in the East. His philosophy of nonviolence and his quest for peace and harmony among individuals and nations is shared by civic actors and public intellectuals around the world. For Martin Luther King, Jr. and His Holiness the Dalai Lama to the young activists of the Tahrir Square and Chinese students in Hong Kong, Gandhi has been the most celebrated and cited political thinker of the twentieth century. Moreover, in the past seventy years Gandhi has been considered as a great figure of dissent, whenever and wherever there has been the question of transition from authoritarianism to democracy or simply the process of democratization of democracy. This is mainly because Gandhi insisted on the creative and transformative role of politics and introduced humanity to the old spiritual art of practising moral courage. That is why Gandhi's nonviolence has been kept alive through its ability to be grasped and practised by other individuals and communities beyond India.

None other than Martin Luther King, Jr. understood well the message of Gandhian nonviolence. It was King who embraced

Gandhian nonviolence as a method of struggle for the emancipation of blacks in America. King's own vision of nonviolence completed that of Gandhi by bringing together the two themes of moral courage and self-suffering. While Gandhi's teachings were based on the two ideas of simple living and truth-seeking, as the means to attain universal harmony among human beings, King insisted on the necessity of a 'cosmic companionship' and the need to build a 'Beloved Community'. Ultimately, King followed Gandhi's path towards nonviolent emancipation of the African-Americans in the United States by giving shape to his own dream of justice and solidarity. The Gandhian philosophy of nonviolence would not have become global had America and the world not recognized the moral courage of Martin Luther King, Jr. and his movement.

4

The Strength of Love

Martin Luther King, Jr. and The Drum Major for Social Justice

If for Gandhi nonviolence was a way of living, for Martin Luther King, Jr. it was certainly a 'drum major instinct'. On 4 February 1968, two months before he was killed by an assassin's bullet on the balcony of the Lorraine Motel in Memphis, King stood before an Ebenezer Baptist Church congregation and gave his sermon on 'The Drum Major Instinct'. It is said, and many times repeated that at this sermon, Martin Luther King, Jr. had a prophetic premonition of his assassination. Near the end of the sermon, King talked about the way he wanted to be remembered on the day of his death.

Every now and then I guess we all think, realistically about that day when we will be victimized with what is life's final common denominator – that something we call death. We all think about it. And every now and then I think about my own death and I think about my own funeral. . . . I'd like somebody to mention that day that Martin Luther King, Jr., tried to give his life serving others. . . . Yes, if you want to say that I was a drum major, say that I was a drum major for justice. Say that I was a drum major for peace. I was a drum major for righteousness.[1]

King's reference to the drum major instinct was not a way for him to glorify himself, but to invite congregants of his church to join him in his quest for peace, love and righteousness. Throughout his active life as a Baptist minister and a civil rights leader, King was committed to service, while fighting against the unjust structures and racist policies of the American society. Yet his practice of nonviolence as a strategy and a mode of thinking turned into a radical quest for a new conception of mutuality, solidarity and interconnectedness in and beyond America. King's critical alertness and his Jesus-like compassion for the suffering of others helped him to become the major protagonist of a new American odyssey against white oppression. However, as King began to speak and to act against segregation in America, he had the genius of bringing together the Christian roots of his emancipatory theology and the Gandhian philosophy of nonviolence.

There has been a great deal of discussion about how King became acquainted with the philosophy of nonviolence. King's introduction to nonviolence began many years before he accepted the call to preach at Dexter Avenue Baptist Church in Montgomery. At the age of nineteen, King graduated from Morehouse College and continued his studies at Crozer Seminary in Pennsylvania. The fact is that Mahatma Gandhi was no stranger at Crozer, and King was not the first liberal-minded student who had been attracted to the Gandhian philosophy of nonviolence. Over the years, in fact, many Crozer graduates had become members of The Fellowship of Reconciliation and The Baptist Pacifist Fellowship. That King was affected more profoundly than others goes without saying. He readily admitted that Gandhi's concept of Satyagraha was 'profoundly significant' for him, and that Gandhi convinced him that love need not be sentimental, nor for weaklings, nor simply applicable to individual relationships, but that whole communities and nations could practise the '"turn-the-other-cheek" philosophy of the Sermon on the Mount'.[2] King was fascinated by Gandhi's proximity to the love ethic of Jesus and his emphasis on nonviolent resistance as a 'method' of life and struggle. But King was also deeply captivated by 'Gandhi's refusal to separate the spiritual and the secular, the religious and the ethical, and the individual and the social'.[3] For King, much more than for Gandhi, nonviolent resistance against injustice and the evil was linked directly to the Christian message of love. King was, first and foremost, a follower of Jesus and his message of neighbourliness, interconnectedness and love in the *Sermon on the Mount*. For King, the aim of nonviolent resistance was to defeat the evil and to glorify divine justice. Justice, rather than law, was the philosophical foundation of King's nonviolent resistance. This is why King often repeated Saint Augustine by affirming that 'An unjust law is no law at all'.[4] According to King, an unjust law is a law which is against the moral code of humanity. An unjust law disregards and discards the otherness of the Other. As a result, an unjust law humiliates and dehumanizes a person, while justice dignifies the human race. This is why King considered racism and segregation as evil. 'All segregation statutes are unjust', affirmed King, 'because segregation distorts the soul and damages the personality. It gives the segregator a false sense of superiority and the segregated a false sense of inferiority.'[5] Therefore, no other subject appeared more frequently in King's speeches, sermons and writings than the obligation to disobey unjust laws and the need to establish a just society. In the exposition of this aspect of nonviolent resistance, King pointed out to what he called the sense of 'somebodiness', that is, the spiritual pride of humankind, which turns him or her into a creature of goodness. That is why 'the nonviolent resister does not seek to humiliate or defeat the opponent but to win his friendship and understanding. This is always a cry that we had to set before people that our aim is not to defeat the white community, not to humiliate the white community, but to win the friendship of all of the persons who had perpetrated this system in the past.'[6]

If one of the contributions of Gandhi to the philosophy of nonviolence was to relate ahimsa to love, that of Martin Luther King, Jr. was to link the two concepts of justice and love. We find this affinity between the two concepts in King's message from the Birmingham jail. He observed,

> Was not Jesus an extremist in love? – 'Love your enemies, bless them that curse you, pray for them that despitefully use you.' Was not Amos an extremist for justice? – 'Let justice roll down like waters and righteousness like a mighty stream.' Was not Paul an extremist for the gospel of Jesus Christ? – 'I bear in my body the marks of the Lord Jesus.' Was not Martin Luther an extremist? – 'Here I stand; I can do no other so help me God.' Was not John Bunyan an extremist? – 'I will stay in jail to the end of my days before I make a mockery of my conscience.'

Was not Abraham Lincoln an extremist? – 'This nation cannot survive half slave and half free.' Was not Thomas Jefferson an extremist? – 'We hold these truths to be self-evident, that all men are created equal.' So the question is not whether we will be extremist, but what kind of extremists we will be. Will we be extremists for hate, or will we be extremists for love? Will we be extremists for the preservation of injustice, or will we be extremists for the cause of justice?[7]

King tried to transform the legitimate social and political discontent of the African-Americans into a creative mass disobedience. However, he was well aware of the fact that in this struggle, the self-transformation of the black community and the transformation of the structures of American society went hand in hand. Depending on the moral and spiritual forces of nonviolent resistance, it seemed clear to King that in any quest for justice integration was a necessary goal. Yet, he did not champion racial justice without also thinking in terms of self-emancipation of the blacks. King was fully conscious that in order to be able to share democratic power with the American whites, African-Americans should learn to see and respect them as citizens and no more as racist slave owners. This is where the teachings of Gandhi and Jesus came to his rescue again. In a discussion with Mayor Gale at the Montgomery City Hall during the famous bus boycott in 1955, King affirmed,

I can see no conflict between our devotion to Jesus Christ and our present action. In fact I see a necessary relationship. If one is truly devoted to the religion of Jesus he will seek to rid the world of social evils. The gospel is social as well as personal. We are only doing in a minor way what Gandhi did in India; and certainly no one referred to him as an unrepentant sinner, he is considered by many a saint.[8]

From King's point of view, the choice between what was considered as the tradition of the African-American community and the ethics of love and nonviolence was clear. For him allegiance to the teachings of Jesus and Gandhi came first. Christianity embodied the prophetic conviction that an ethical life is the best way to serve God, while the Gandhian philosophy of *Satyagraha* was based on the nonviolent process of applying the spiritual to the sphere of action. As Smith and Zepp underline correctly in *Search for the Beloved Community*,

> the general theme of Gandhi's thought which struck a responsive chord in King after two years of study of evangelical liberalism and the Social Gospel was Gandhi's refusal to separate the spiritual and the secular, the religious and the ethical, and the individual and the social. Gandhi combined a deeply religious faith with an intense social involvement. . . . We find the same blend of the religious and the social in King's life and writing.[9]

Here, King's emphasis on the spiritualization of the political is significant because it indicates that his nonviolent resistance against racism and injustice in America was a strategy of Gandhian nature, rather than a simple act of passive pacifism. By this emphasis, King attempted to establish the fact that his nonviolence, like that of Jesus and Gandhi, was rooted in the moral courage of seeking the Truth and facing the evil, and was the method of the strongest. King went to great lengths to describe the struggle of black nonviolent resisters in the American society as a virtue far from fear and anger. According to him, the struggle of the black Americans for social change was essentially inscribed in the transforming possibilities of suffering. 'My personal trials have taught me the value of unmerciful sufferings,' he wrote in the *Christian Century*. 'If only to save myself from bitterness, I have attempted to see my personal ordeals as an opportunity to transcend myself and heal the people involved in the tragic situation that now obtains.'[10]

King had a great historical responsibility thrust upon him from which he could not turn away. He understood this truth from the very beginning of the bus boycott campaign in Montgomery, from 5 December 1955 to 20 December 1956. There were many parallels between the Montgomery bus boycott and Gandhi's nonviolent resistance in India. As Stephen Oates underlines,

> What Gandhi accomplished there – freedom and justice without a legacy of bitterness – was precisely what King desired here in Montgomery. With the help of several pacifists and Christian socialists, who hurried to Montgomery to contribute ideas about Gandhi and nonviolent direct action, King set about fashioning a philosophy for the bus protest, one that derived largely from the social philosophy he had forged at Crozer and Boston University. Here at last was a chance to translate his own theoretical concepts into practical action.[11]

Though King took many of his cues from Gandhi's strategy of nonviolence, he continued to be faithful to the Christian doctrine of love and justice. When King talked about the moral law of the universe, he had the divine justice in mind. As King said, 'Even though the arc of the moral universe is long, but it bends towards justice.'[12] King shaped his moral vision of love on the divine nature of justice in the cosmos. King distinguished between three different types of love: *Eros, Philia and Agape*. He referred to *Eros* as romantic love; to *Philia* as friendly love; and to *Agape* as a disinterested love. According to him, resistance to evil was possible only with this third type of love. Agape was the only avenue to both transforming oneself and respecting the dignity of the other. As King proclaimed,

> Agape means nothing sentimental or basically affectionate; it means understanding, redeeming good will for all men, an overflowing love which seeks nothing in return. It is the love of God working in the lives of men. When we love on the Agape level we love men not because we like them, not because their attitudes and ways appeal to us, but because God loves them. Here we rise to the position of loving the person who does the evil deed while hating the deed he does.[13]

Moreover, according to King, the function of Agape love is to support the community. Through the practice of Agape love, King tried to achieve a Beloved Community, where blacks and whites could coexist. His central idea was to encourage the blacks and the whites to commit themselves to the task of reconciliation and preserving the community. Therefore, 'the connection made between love and community was an element of one of King's fundamental theological assumptions: all life is a part of a single process; all men are brothers. One cannot do good or harm to another person without both parties being affected.'[14] Ultimately, for King, the Beloved Community had to be just and compassionate. In other words, the laws should be just and reflect the moral law of the universe. That is to say, as stated previously, in King's philosophy of nonviolence the ethic of love and the provision of justice should go hand in hand. This was necessary not only because King considered the Beloved Community as an ideal expression of Christian love, but also because it represented for him a regenerated broken community. That is to say, in a Beloved Community, citizens were fully conscious about the otherness of the Other and this awareness guided them towards a degree of maturity and interdependency.

> King interpreted the interrelatedness of human existence to mean that 'injustice anywhere is a threat to justice everywhere' because injustice has a corporate effect. He believed that the denial of constitutional rights to anyone potentially violated the rights of all citizens. . . . As a result of his solidaristic approach to human existence King believed that the civil rights movement was contributing more to the national life than simply the elimination of racial injustice.[15]

As such, King envisioned nonviolence as both struggle and compassion. He wanted people to be compassionate to their adversaries in the same way as they are to their family and friends. If the universe was just and righteous, then behind the struggle for righteousness resided what King called a 'cosmic companionship'.[16] So in the truest sense of the word, King's principle of nonviolence was based on the idea that the world is a home for all human beings. The vision of interrelatedness was, therefore, the organizing philosophical principle of all of King's thoughts and practices. All of King's intellectual concerns were directed to the priority he assigned to the idea of recognition of one's responsibility and indebtedness to others. As King later wrote:

We are everlasting debtors to known and unknown men and women. We do not finish breakfast without being dependent on more than half of the world. When we arise in the morning, we go into the bathroom where we reach for a sponge which is provided for us by a Pacific Islander. We reach for soap that is created for us by a Frenchman. The towel is provided by a Turk. Then at the table we drink coffee which is provided for us by a South American, or tea by a Chinese, or cocoa by a West African. Before we leave for our jobs we are beholden to more than half the world. In a real sense, all life is interrelated. All men are caught in an inescapable network of mutuality, tied in a single garment of destiny. Whatever affects one directly affects all indirectly.[17]

King's appreciation of indebtedness and interconnectedness was directly linked to the challenge of injustice in the world and the relief of the suffering of others around the world. That is why he repudiated the moral legitimacy of a state which conquered the others. Therefore, while being a true cosmopolitan thinker, King moved against the narrowness and violence of American nationalism. His celebrated 'Beyond Vietnam' speech given at the Riverside Church in New York was a public condemnation of the American involvement in Southeast Asia. 'I don't believe', declared King, 'we can have world peace until America has an "integrated" foreign policy. Our disastrous experiences in Vietnam and the Dominican Republic have been, in one sense, a result of racist decision-making.'[18] The manner in which King criticized the war in Vietnam was closely related to his approach concerning the transformation of the social, political and economic structures of injustice in the American society. King realized that all Americans, whether black or white, were responsible for their shameless indifference towards the misery of others. Therefore, according to him, the battle for democracy and civil rights in America was directly linked with the demand for the end of war in Vietnam. In the eyes of King, the dignity of a Vietnamese child killed by an American soldier was not less than an African-American suffering from poverty in Harlem or in Alabama. He explained,

> What must they think of the United States of America when they realize that we permitted the repression and cruelty of Diem, which helped to bring them into being as a resistance group in the South? What do they think of our condoning the violence which led to their own taking up of arms? How can they believe in our integrity when now we speak of 'aggression from the North' as if there was nothing more essential to the war? How can they trust us when now we charge them with violence after the murderous reign of Diem and charge them with violence while we pour every new weapon of death into their land?[19]

King believed that Americans needed to protest not only the war in Vietnam, but also militarism in general. According to him, Americans needed to recognize and fight the three evils of racism, extreme materialism and militarism. Calling on Americans to transform their society, King insisted on a true 'revolution of values'. King's new approach to nonviolence was based on the conviction that resistance against unjust laws is also bottom-up solidarity and a long work for social and political transformation. Thus, King was thinking in terms of a process of questioning the fairness of institutions and redefining the American democracy. This new praxis of dissent was not only a new approach to power without sovereignty, what Vaclav Havel two decades later called the 'power of the powerless', but also the emergence of a clear perspective of compromise as an act of 'coming together' and 'making a mutual promise'. Thus the task for Martin Luther King, Jr. was to renew the civic philosophy of dissent by overcoming the division between ethics and politics. King's actions in Montgomery, Selma, Washington D.C., Memphis and elsewhere were the exemplifications of his innovative project of nonviolent dissent and the demonstration of the fact that there could be no approach to political life without an appeal to the ethical. King felt strongly about Thoreau and Gandhi, not only because he considered them in the same line of dissenting revolt against injustice, but because he put his faith in the belief that the Gandhian realistic approach to the praxis of nonviolence and Thoreau's self-transformative art of disobedience could very well go hand in hand and provide a sphere of enlarged citizenship. Consequently, King brought the Gandhian principle of spiritual self-transformation into conversation with the challenges of interrelatedness in America and beyond by affirming:

The large house in which we live demands that we transform this world-wide neighborhood into a world-wide brotherhood. Together we must learn to live as brothers or together we will be forced to perish as fools. . . . We must work passionately and indefatigably to bridge the gulf between our scientific progress and our moral progress. One of the great problems of mankind is that we suffer from a poverty of the spirit which stands in glaring contrast to our scientific and technological abundance. The richer we have become materially, the poorer we have become morally and spiritually.[20]

Martin Luther King's theory of political empathy went far beyond the simple neighbourly care for others. As discussed previously, King's nonviolence demanded full transformation of self and others. Through his struggles and writings, King insisted that Americans cultivate a sense of the otherness of the Other beyond one's greatness in terms of individual achievements. In part due to his concern with the otherness of the Other (i.e., with transforming blacks and whites in the American society), King can be considered as a resolute supporter of what we can call an 'empathetic nonviolence'. Ultimately, for King, nonviolence would be summarized in the work of individuals and the law of the heart rather than the dynamic of social and political institutions. As King observed in *Where Do We Go From Here: Chaos or Community?*: 'I am concerned that Negroes achieve full status as citizens and as human beings here in the United States. But I am also concerned about our moral uprightness and the health of our souls.'[21] What King is arguing here is that true reconciliation can be achieved only by not repeating the past. King invited the African-Americans to look the beast of violence in the eye, without driving out the hate of the beast with a new hate. As such, with the moral clarity born out of his experiments with nonviolence, King showed his fellow Americans how to move forward with compassion to build a more humane society. King knew well that hate and revenge were elements of a time bomb that could explode at any time, rendering the new values of the Beloved Community vulnerable. He, therefore, opted to wipe out the last vestiges of racism from the American society. But as in the case of Gandhi and his Constructive Programme, King stepped into a worldwide war against poverty. He suggested that the aid programmes be galvanized by compassion and empathy and be put into action by a spirit of mutual understanding. Returning to his philosophy of self and other, King proclaimed:

> I would say that other-preservation is the first law of life. It is the first law of life precisely because we cannot preserve self without being concerned about preserving other selves. The universe is so structured that things go awry if men are not diligent in their cultivation of the other-regarding dimension. 'I' cannot reach fulfillment without 'thou.' The self cannot be self without other selves. Self-concern without other-concern is like a tributary that has no outward flow to the ocean. Stagnant, still and stale, it lacks both life and freshness. Nothing would be more disastrous and out of harmony with our self-interest than for the developed nations to travel a dead-end road of inordinate selfishness.[22]

King was quite aware of the fact that a deep sense of morality and nonviolent resistance could not mingle with an egoistic and self-centred subject which undermines the otherness of the Other. If anything, King was a man of experimentation, a man who insisted on the quest for love and justice. Therefore, it should not come as a surprise to us that his dream, far from being a utopian dream, was a search for a more just and harmonious society. The victory of the civil rights movement in the United States was a proof positive of the truth of this dream coming true. By promoting the dynamic of nonviolence that he learned from the teachings of Jesus Christ and Mahatma Gandhi, Martin Luther King, Jr. was able to rehabilitate and reaffirm the dignity and personhood of the African-Americans, who for so long had been silenced and dehumanized by the white America. But there was more to King which made him a political thinker and a relevant social reformer. King was a dialogical thinker who was open to other horizons of thinking. He firmly believed that the spirit of genuine reciprocity and solidarity is not just a moral requirement, but also a political necessity. That is why King rejected the idea of nationalism. He believed that American democracy matters, but even more, because he was of the opinion that humanity matters. Thus, King was convinced about the fact that a nation which is incapable of changing its norms and values is a truncated form of nation. He, therefore, established a relationship between the moral dynamic for the survival of the American Dream and the dynamic of a global revolution of values. Finally, his nonviolence encouraged inter-religious and intercultural dialogue, so that individuals, who were in the quest for truth, love and justice, could see their faith and culture in comparison with that of the other. In other words, he made a call for simultaneous awareness of commonalities, acceptance of differences and recognition of shared values. As such, King was not alien at all to the intercultural nature of nonviolent resistance in the world. For a long time, he had preached that the revolution of values should also take place outside the American context.

'A true revolution of values', he wrote in his *Autobiography*, will soon look uneasily on the glaring contrast of poverty and wealth. With righteous indignation, it will look across the seas and see individual capitalists of the West investing huge sums of money in Asia, Africa, and South America, only to take the profits out with no concern for the social betterment of the countries and say: 'This is not just.' It will look at our alliance with the landed gentry of South America and say, 'This is not just.' The Western arrogance of feeling that it has everything to teach others and nothing to learn from them is not just.[23]

In the manner of Gandhi, King was a great leader of nonviolence, but he also knew how to listen and learn before leading his flock. Interestingly, King was a civil society leader and a social practitioner who was constantly reading, learning and experimenting with different epistemologies of resistance. King's exposure to the ideas of Reinhold Niehbur and Walter Rauschenbusch made him aware of the complexity of sin on every level of man's existence. His discovery of the emancipatory theology was followed by his intellectual adventures in reading philosophers like Hegel, Marx, Nietzsche and Kierkegaard. All these influences made him understand that the 'moral pilgrimage' of humankind may bring it closer to the 'city of righteousness'.[24] Similar but also different, King and Gandhi were united in their moral and political dreams of changing humanity. As a dreamer, King looked for a harmonious universe, where the forces of evil, and especially violence, would be defeated with the help of God. But as a pragmatist who had a devastating sense of reality, he was a fox who knew that the insane world of human beings is filled with hatred, revenge, greed for power and violence. King knew that nonviolence could not achieve miracles overnight, but it could change the hearts and minds of those engaged with it. He said famously, 'the aftermath of nonviolence is the creation of the beloved community, while the aftermath of violence is tragic bitterness.'[25] This is a historical lesson that Nelson Mandela and Vaclav Havel understood in their own historical contexts. They both worked unceasingly for the realization of societies where reconciliation, forgiveness and transition to democracy would replace systems of violence, hatred, lies and dehumanization. The reflections of Desmond Tutu, a very important practitioner of nonviolence, are crucial in showing us how a common experience of nonviolent resistance and reconciliation helps us to build a more humane world. As he observed in his book *No Future Without Forgiveness*,

It is crucial too that we keep remembering that negotiations, peace talks, forgiveness, and reconciliation happen most frequently not between friends, not between those who like one another. They happen precisely because people are at loggerheads and detest one another as only enemies can. But enemies are potential allies, friends, colleagues, and collaborators. This is not just utopian idealism. The first democratically-elected government of South Africa was a government of National Unity made up of members of political parties that were engaged in a life-and-death struggle. The man who headed it had been incarcerated for twenty-seven years as a dangerous terrorist. If it could happen there, surely it can happen in other places. Perhaps God chose such an unlikely place deliberately to show the world that it can be done anywhere.[26]

5

Reconciliation and Negotiation

Nelson Mandela and Vaclav Havel

It would be incorrect and inaccurate to search for a Mahatma Gandhi or a Martin Luther King, Jr. in either Nelson Mandela or Vaclav Havel. Neither Mandela nor Havel was a principled nonviolent leader with a very strong belief or opinion concerning the philosophy of nonviolent resistance. However, they are both representatives of a moral political leadership, which did not separate between politics and ethics in the name of a Machiavellian realism or a Leninist vanguardism.

Nelson Mandela was a man who cherished the ideal of a free society all his life, an ideal that, as he proclaimed at his trial in Pretoria in April 1964, he hoped to live for, and if need be, die for. During his lifetime Mandela dedicated himself to the freedom struggle of the African people. To do this, he fought against white and black dominations in South Africa. But more than anything else he fought for democracy as a plural society in which all persons of all races, languages and opinions can live together in harmony and with equal opportunity. However, what Nelson Mandela as a political and moral leader made possible for humanity was extending and expanding our capacity to rethink politics in terms of an ethics of empathy, a politics of forgiveness and a revolution of values in South Africa. As such, Mandela was not necessarily, as he proclaimed later, 'an ordinary man who became a leader because of extraordinary circumstances'.[1] Truly speaking, the South African transition to democracy, under the leadership of Mandela, was a great work of political creativity and moral wisdom. As a matter of fact, the two famous definitions of a human being by Aristotle, that he is a political being and a being endowed with speech, supplement each other in Mandela's anti-Apartheid practice of freedom. What Mandela understood through his life experience was that freedom cannot be speechless, while violence is incapable of speech. That such an outspokenness (what the ancient Greeks called *parrhesia*) must be intimately connected with the ideal of freedom seems to be vouched for by the legendary life of Mandela himself. Mandela's life experience speaks clearly for itself: the transformation of Mandela himself and that of the South African society went hand in hand.

Mandela was born more than a hundred years ago in a world where outspokenness was not practised among blacks in South Africa. 'We were meant to learn through imitation and emulation, not through asking questions,'[2] he wrote in his autobiography entitled *Long Walk to Freedom*. Yet, Mandela enjoyed a place of honour through his line of descent in the Thembu chieftaincy. Though sent to the Methodist mission schools in the Eastern Cape and later to the University of Fort

Hare, Mandela's interests and ambitions at this point were to become a court interpreter. Surprisingly, and in contrast to other students who attended Fort Hare, Mandela's commitment to African politics was much more undecided and uncertain. There are many conflicting interpretations in relation to the early stages of Mandela's life, but all Mandela's biographers agree that the important development in his political life began after his arrival in Johannesburg. At this point, Mandela put his rural experience in Transkei behind him and made up his mind to engage himself in politics.

Interestingly Mandela's political future as a national leader was established and solidified by two facts: the bus boycott of 1943 in Alexandra and his meeting with Walter Sisulu, who was an African nationalist. 'Walter's house in Orlando', Mandela wrote later, 'was a Mecca for activists and ANC members.'[3] These two influences drove Mandela to form the ANC Youth League in 1944. However, the young Mandela proved to be a much more inflexible Africanist than many of his colleagues in the Youth League. Regarding this period, Mandela observes in *Conversations with Myself*: 'I must be frank and tell you that when I look back at some of my early writings and speeches I am appalled by their pedantry, artificiality and lack of originality.'[4]

In a sense, Mandela's political lifestyle and his political thinking did not really start to evolve before the 1950s. It is after he established a legal practice in 1952 with his fellow lawyer and ANC executive member Oliver Tambo that his self-confidence grew enormously and changed his lifestyle and his political leadership. The next two turning points in Mandela's private life and his political struggle were his marriage with his second wife, Winnie Madikizela, and the Sharpeville Massacre in March 1960, when a hundred African demonstrators were killed, and both the African National Congress (ANC) and the Pan-African Congress (PAC) were banned. This was the moment when Mandela decided to go underground and create a new military organization, *Umkhonto we Sizwe* (Spear of the Nation). From Nelson Mandela's point of view the political necessity which forced him and his comrades to create the military organization *Umkhonto we Sizwe* in the early 1960s was not a pure celebration of violence. For Mandela, ANC's exit from nonviolence and the choice of non-lethal sabotage was a bitter confession that 'fifty years of nonviolence had brought the African people nothing but more repressive legislation, and fewer and fewer rights'.[5] But Mandela's vision of a new South Africa did not stop there. Despite the temporary exit of ANC from the principles of nonviolence, he continued to believe in the two concepts of negotiation and reconciliation. In the eyes of Mandela, the choice of turning ANC into a violent organization was to acquire the best hope of reconciliation afterwards. Nevertheless, Mandela was the first to criticize his decision of establishing *Umkhonto* later in the mid-1970s. He wrote the following while he was in prison: 'We had made exactly that mistake, drained the political organizations of their enthusiastic and experienced men, concentrated our attention on the new organization.'[6] Mandela was not a direct actor in any of the non-lethal acts of sabotage, but he was not followed in his decision by some influential members of the ANC like Oliver Tambo. In any case, Mandela's clandestine travels inside and outside the South African territory ended with his arrest on 4 July 1961 at Howick, on the road from Durban to Johannesburg.

At his famous Rivonia trial, Mandela insisted on ANC's heritage of nonviolence and racial harmony and delivered his historical speech which received sympathetic treatment around the world. On 12 June

1962, Judge de Wet pronounced life imprisonment for Mandela and his fellow prisoners. From that day on Mandela lived for twenty-seven years and six months in captivity. More than seventeen years of this sentence was spent on Robben Island as prisoner 466/64. However, as he wrote later, prison gave him plenty of time 'to stand back and look at the entire movement from a distance'.[7] He revised his views and values, while keeping his moral authority and his capacities for political judgement.

Nelson Mandela walked out of the Victor Verster prison at 4.14 pm on 11 February 1990, but his march to freedom still had some way to go. The second memorable moment of his life and that of the South African nation was when he was elected on 27 April 1994 as South Africa's first democratic president. As such, 'Madiba', as Mandela was called (this was his clan name), accomplished his heroic and messianic status by having met the challenges of his life and those of his time. Whether as an activist, as a prisoner or as a leader in government, Nelson Mandela remained intensely conscious of his moral and political responsibilities as a man in search for excellence. Even after he died on 5 December 2013 at his home in Houghton, he remained a national and international figure with a legacy of politics of excellence. As Mandela's life and struggles reveal, his search for excellence in politics was far from being simply a pacifist. Yet, Mandela was very different from all other African anti-colonial leaders and resisters, especially Frantz Fanon, who believed that the use of violence had a healing power over the colonized people. As Jonathan Hyslop observes, it would be wrong to portray Mandela 'as oscillating between a violent Fanonism and a peaceful Gandhianism'.[8] But, it is important to recognize that Mandela's idea of the use of violence was not a case of conscience, but a political calculation which symbolized a key period of his struggle against the Apartheid regime. Surprisingly, 'although the peaceful campaigns of the ANC in the early 1950s were modeled on Indian *satyagraha* principles, Mandela was much more attracted by the pragmatic Nehru (who by then had already led India in a major war) than the utopian Gandhi. And as his radicalization proceeded, he began to contemplate violent resistance.'[9] One might not hear that Mandela's approach to Gandhi and his nonviolence always stood as a tactic and never as a principle. He explained this political attitude in *Conversations with Myself*:

> We took up the attitude that we would stick to nonviolence only insofar as the conditions permitted that. Once the conditions were against that we would automatically abandon nonviolence and use the methods which were dictated by the conditions. That was our approach. Our approach was to empower the organisation to be effective in its leadership. And if the adoption of nonviolence gave it that effectiveness, that efficiency, we would pursue nonviolence. But if the condition shows that nonviolence was not effective, we would use other means.[10]

As it was underlined previously, while thinking in terms of Clausewitz and war or reading Che Guevara on guerilla warfare, Mandela had the idea of reconciliation in the back of his mind. He was not in search of constructing a new African dictatorship. He, therefore, started studying his enemies and engaged in a constructive dialogue with his warders.

He recognized that when the prisoners had a good relationship with warders who dealt with them, 'it became difficult for the higher-ups to treat you roughly' . . . He was always hopeful of converting them and said, 'I soon realized that when an Afrikaner changes, he changes completely and becomes a real friend.' [Interestingly] Sisulu saw these talks as the precursor to the eventual discussions with the government.[11]

An important premise of such readiness for dialogue was that Mandela and his ANC fellow prisoners realized gradually that the path of violence had failed. Once again, Mandela accepted the fact that choosing violence had 'drained the political organizations of their enthusiastic and experienced men'.[12]

Now, once again, what distinguished Mandela as a moral leader from ordinary politicians with no moral capital was the absence of bitterness and vengeance in him, which was certainly central to what came later in South Africa. It is so interesting that while preserving his dignity as a prisoner and as a political leader, he never tried to humiliate his political opponents. Accordingly, Mandela accumulated his moral capital as a leader through his empathetic ethics and with a self-conscious respect for the otherness of the Other. That is why, then, there were certainly moments and phases in Mandela's life when his character as a moral leader and as a democratic hero came closer to the Gandhian ideal of a nonviolent *Satyagrahi*. It is with this Gandhian spirit in mind that Mandela accepted to join hands with his enemies in order to drag South Africa out of hatred and bloodshed. As he affirmed, 'All South Africans must now unite and join hands and say we are one country, one nation, one people, marching together into the future.'[13] Let us not forget that Mandela was brought up with the African philosophy of *ubuntu* which described a quality of empathy and compassion. 'It was therefore not surprising that when Mandela assumed the presidency in 1994, South Africa's foreign policy continued the legacy formulated by the older generation and was defined by the notion of "a better Africa and a better world." Mandela prioritized these fundamental *ubuntu*-inspired values as essential to cultivating a humane foreign policy.'[14] Yet, Mandela's *ubuntesque* behaviour did not always give rise to comprehensive approvals, especially in cases of reconciliation and forgiveness of Apartheid political assassins. But Mandela's gestures of civic nationalism and inter-racial dialogue, especially during the Rugby World Cup of 1995 in South Africa and its centrality to the project of nation-building, were reminders of the Gandhian moments of communal harmony beyond the work of ideologies and political parties.

As Mandela's political life shows us, different strategies of nonviolence became ideals for which Nelson Mandela was ready to live or die, but not kill. Despite all his critics on the Right, and his Marxist adulators on the Left, who try to distance him from nonviolence, one needs to know that Mandela never abandoned Gandhi or King. There are many more references in his *Autobiography* to Mahatma Gandhi and Martin Luther King, Jr. than to Che Guevara or Lenin. Even during his visit to Harlem, New York, on 21 June 1990, he quoted Martin Luther King's famous speech: 'Free at last, free at last, thank God Almighty we are free at last.' Mandela and King never met, but they fought for nonviolence at the same time on two different continents. Both Mandela and King read Gandhi and were influenced differently by him, but they practised his philosophy of nonviolent resistance differently. If Mandela is celebrated today as a leader with a moral capital, rather than a pure Gandhian, it is mainly because his politics of dialogue and reconciliation is more relevant than ever for all those who continue to believe in the nonviolent pursuit of public happiness and in the actions of human beings engaged in governing themselves. This is also what Vaclav Havel believed in.

Unlike Nelson Mandela, Vaclav Havel was no leader of an opposition party in Czechoslovakia. He was a playwright and an artist, before being a civic activist. As in the case of Mandela it would be difficult to consider Havel as a pure Gandhian. However, though Havel and Gandhi were men of different times, they drew upon similar principles in their quests for freedom and truth. With a little effort in studying their writings and speeches, it can be shown that there are many similarities between the two leaders. As a matter of fact, both Havel and Gandhi established a close connection between ethics and politics in their social and political philosophy. If for Gandhi, experiments with politics had a fundamental ethical premise, finding its major exemplifications in the values of responsibility, civility and tolerance, for Havel political action was also marked by notions such as 'truth' and 'conscience'. Havel's emphasis on the acknowledgement of truth as an essential value arose from his concern with what he calls 'living in truth' in a post-totalitarian state. As Michael Žantovský explains in his biography of Havel, for the Czech president, the distinction

> between the totalitarian system, as practiced by Stalin and Hitler at the height of their power, and the post-totalitarian system, as practiced by Husak's 'normalizers' in the mid-seventies, does not lie merely in the considerably smaller amount of violence and

brute force exerted by the latter. By soliciting empty expressions of popular support, the system obviates the sharp distinction between the 'tyrants' and the 'victims', which is characteristic of pure dictatorships.[15]

According to Havel, 'Individuals . . . need not accept the lie. It is enough for them to have accepted their life with it and in it. For by this very fact, individuals confirm the system, fulfill the system, make the system, are the system.'[16] As Havel puts it succinctly here, the overwhelming problem is to confront political power by inviting people to live in truth and justice, and for decency. Havel shows brilliantly how the system successfully captures the lived experience of individuals in a post-totalitarian state by giving them the illusion of being part of a silent contract.

But the real sphere of potential politics in the post-totalitarian system is elsewhere: in the continuing and cruel tension between the complex demands of that system and the aims of life, that is, the elementary need of human beings to live, to a certain extent at least, in harmony with themselves, that is, to live in a bearable way, not to be humiliated by their superiors and officials, not to be continually watched by the police, to be able to express themselves freely, to find an outlet for their creativity, to enjoy legal security, and so on.[17]

For Havel, an embryonic act of dissent is not to become a player in the game of a post-totalitarian state, while defending one's dignity and regaining one's sense of responsibility. This is clearly a moral act, which is defined by Havel as 'living within truth'. Havel analyzes the essence of living within truth while examining the various dimensions of what he calls 'the power of the powerless'. He writes,

> When I speak of living within truth, I naturally do not have in mind only products of conceptual thought, such as a protest or a letter written by a group of intellectuals. It can be any means by which a person or a group revolts against manipulation: anything from a letter by intellectuals to a workers' strike, from a rock concert to a student demonstration, from refusing to vote in the farcical elections, to making an open speech at some official congress, or even a hunger strike, for instance. If the suppression of the aims of life is a complex process, and if it is based on the multifaceted manipulation of all expressions of life then, by the same token, every free expression of life indirectly threatens the post-totalitarian system politically, including forms of expression to which, in other social systems, no one would attribute any potential political significance, not to mention explosive power.[18]

The strategies of nonviolent resistance, dissent and non-cooperation suggested by Havel are presented by him as different ontological modes of living within truth. Interestingly, *the Gandhian* philosophy of *satyagraha* is also a logical and ethical outcome of holding on to truth. As we saw previously, for Gandhi, satyagraha is an instrument of nonviolent public dissent and a pragmatic tool of the powerless against the powerful. However, while being an instrument of non-cooperation and civic opposition, satyagraha is also, essentially, a highly moral and spiritual tool. Gandhi's theory of satyagraha implies, first and foremost, an abiding commitment to the soul force of a person who chooses an ethical course of action in the most immoral environment.

As he mentions, 'The only condition of a successful use of this force is a recognition of the existence of the soul as apart from the body and its permanent nature. And this recognition must amount to a living faith and not mere intellectual grasp.'[19] After all, from Gandhi's point of view, satyagrahic action is an appeal to one's own conscience, where the ethical principles are overpowered in contradistinction to the meaning of an incomplete conventional political power.

As pointed out previously, there is an ethical dimension to Havel's political philosophy which echoes Gandhi's moral dimension of politics. Though he was not a religious person, one can find, clearly and transparently, in Havel's writings, concepts such as conscience, transcendence, and Being. 'In this endeavor lies, for Havel, the "existential revolution" carried by a specific form of "communality" of "love, charity, sympathy, tolerance, understanding, self-control, solidarity, friendship . . ."'[20] Moreover, Havel's call to concepts such as conscience and belief attributes a more spiritual foundation to his civic humanism. Perhaps the best example of this appears in *Summer Meditations*, where Havel affirms: 'Acting sensitively in a situation does not exclude morality, but is more likely to accompany it, be bound to it, and even derive from it, because it comes from the same source – responsible thinking, attentiveness, and a dialogue with one's own conscience.'[21] Havel also greatly emphasizes the establishment of a relationship between democracy and the spiritual in his famous essay, 'Politics, Morality and Civility': 'I am convinced that we will never build a democratic state built on rule of law if we do not at the same time build a state that is – regardless of how unscientific this may sound to the ears of a political scientist – humane, moral, intellectual and spiritual, and cultural.'[22] It is therefore undeniable that the kind of democratic system envisaged by Havel is born out of a sentiment of responsibility and solidarity with the suffering humanity, which can clearly be translated into a Gandhian grammar of 'spiritualization of politics'. Although not a true practitioner of religion, Havel refers very often in his writings and speeches to the 'mysterious memory of Being' or to 'the spirit of Christian morality'. In his famous speech, 'Welcome to the Visit of the Pope John Paul II at Prague Castle in April 1990', Havel develops his own idea of spirituality:

> I strongly believe that your visit will remind us all of the genuine source of real human responsibility, its metaphysical source. I strongly believe that your visit will remind us of what we need so much to be reminded of today: the absolute horizon to which we must refer, that mysterious memory of Being in which each of our acts is recorded and in which and through which they finally acquire their true value. I strongly believe that face to face with Your Holiness, we shall realize that above our earthly world of day-to-day toil there is something which from time immemorial has been called heaven. History in our country ceased to flow against the current of conscience. Let us not allow it be it under whatever banner to flow that way again. I welcome you, Holy Father, among us sinners.[23]

One year before delivering this speech, in his conversations with Karel Hvížďala, entitled *Disturbing the Peace*, Havel emphasized the need to recognize the notion of 'belief' as an essential value in life. 'Whatever the case may be', underlines Havel,

> I consider myself a believer only in the sense in which I used the word in my letters: I believe that all of this – life and the universe –

is not just 'in and of itself'. I believe that nothing disappears forever, and less so our deeds, which is why I believe that it makes sense to try to do something in life, something more than that which will bring one obvious returns. . . . I can try to live in the spirit of Christian morality (not very successfully, it's true), but that doesn't mean that I'm a genuinely believing Christian. I'm just not certain that Christ is the Son of God and a god-man, not just figuratively (as a kind of archetype of man), but in the profound and binding way that it holds true for a Christian.[24]

Though it would be wrong to describe Havel's political philosophy as purely Gandhian, it goes without saying that there are many similarities between his anthropological optimism based on commonly shared moral values and that of Gandhi. For Havel, as for Gandhi, politics is not only the 'practice of morality', it is also a space which should be understood in terms of decency. Havel puts it well: 'I am happy to leave political intrigue to others; I will not compete with them, certainly not by using their weapons. Genuine politics worthy of the name, and the only politics I am willing to devote myself to is simply a matter of serving those around us: serving the community, and serving those who will come after us. Its deepest roots are moral because it is a responsibility, expressed through action, to and for the whole, a responsibility that is what it is – a "higher" responsibility – only because it has a metaphysical grounding.'[25] This genuine Gandhian concern for the common good in the work of Havel reminds us of the inherent fragility of human existence and the frailty of the human political condition. Therein lies the ethical interrogation of Havel who was confronted with the realism of political power. Until the very last moment of his life, Václav Havel embraced the Gandhian ethics of responsibility and his commitment to human dignity, while not fully supporting Gandhi's moral injunction to be nonviolent in deed and in action. Havel acted along the lines of nonviolence all his life, though he did not reject the idea of violent methods in global affairs when he concluded that nonviolence yielded no results. According to Žantovský, many people thought that Havel, like Gandhi,

> had absolutely sworn off the use of violence, and they would be disappointed later when Havel, by then president, turned out not to be a pacifist after all. . . . Havel's staunch advocacy of interventions in former Yugoslavia and Kosovo, and even more so his later open support for the effort to remove Saddam Hussein (rather than for the method of his removal), came at a price, tainting his idealized image as a saintly patron of nonviolence. But it is the image rather than the man that is at issue here: Havel, like Gandhi and Mandela, was advocating nonviolence not only as a matter of moral principle but as a weapon of political struggle. Havel would always give precedence to a peaceful and amicable way of conflict resolution but he believed too strongly in the inadmissibility of appeasement when facing an evil to be a pacifist.[26]

Let us not forget that even if Havel was very loyal to the Czech Republic and to the Czechs, his responsibility as a moral leader made him speak the truth beyond the national and cultural frontiers by picking the right moral and political alternative, and then wisely representing it where it could do the best and cause the right change. Havel's attitude towards nonviolent construction and education of the Czech society was based on his idea of what he called a 'higher responsibility'. As he wrote in the Afterword of *Summer Meditations*,

> My political career too was, in the beginning, just a 'filling in', something for which I personally feel little need, and which I see more as a burden than as a delight. What am I to do in this situation? It would seem that only now has the time come for a really serious decision. Should I return to work as a writer? Or should I remain in practical politics and let my name stand once more for the presidential office? I have been thinking about this decision for a long time, and it presents me with a genuine dilemma. There are so many arguments for and against. The longer I think about it, the more clearly I come to realize that this dilemma is essentially just a new and particularly acute form of the same one I have faced throughout my adult life. Should I put myself and my personal interests first? That is, should I put the tranquil, less public, and certainly less exhausting life of an independent intellectual first? Or should I listen to the voice of 'higher responsibility', which is constantly whispering in my ear that the work is far from done and that it is my duty to continue?[27]

Havel played an important role in the Velvet Revolution of 1989 in Czechoslovakia. The Velvet Revolution (sametová revoluce) was a nonviolent transition of power in what was then Czechoslovakia. The Czech experience of democracy has shown that democratization in Eastern Europe took place less within the framework of the existing state systems than at the level of civil societies. When the Czech dissidents of the 1980s were struggling against their communist authoritarian regimes, they returned to the concept of civil society.

What Eastern European intellectuals and civic actors understood by civil society was not just the eighteenth-century concept of the rule of law, but also the notion of horizontal self-organized groups and institutions in the public sphere that could limit the power of the state by constructing a democratic space separate from state and its ideological institutions. Before 1989 and the rise of liberal values in Eastern Europe, many observers argued about the weakness of the civil societies in the region. This perspective forgot two things. First, the sheer ruthlessness of communist regimes that refused civic dissent any room to manoeuvre: no free trade unions, no real opposition, no free press, no tolerance of even a hint of dissidence. Second, the miracle that stubborn civil societies did persist in countries like Poland and Czechoslovakia – even after decades of Stalinist rule, students, intellectuals and artists continued their work and helped to lay the ground for the democratic revolt.

Moreover, the Czech experience showed us that even within a totalitarian society, a basis for 'civic pluralism' can be created. Although other forms of civility existed in East European societies, this civic pluralism – with roots in a philosophical reading of pluralism, in opposition to ideological 'monism'– offered a rich model for those dissidents seeking to make democratic change sustainable. Not surprisingly, Vaclav Havel and other dissidents in Czechoslovakia opened spaces for new civil and democratic politics in Eastern Europe. Charter 77, the Czechoslovak manifesto for human rights, issued in January 1977 by Havel, Jan Patocka and Jiri Hájek, paved the way for the events of the 'Velvet Revolution' of 17 November 1989. In thinking about the Velvet Revolution of 1989, one wonders whether existing paradigms are even adequate, or if new ones are required to make sense of this landmark event. Thirty years later, we still need to ask about the nature of its vision and the scope of its demands. Was it reformist or revolutionary, or perhaps 'refolutionary' as Timothy Garton Ash had suggested?[28] The truth is that Havel and all those involved in the movement of 1989 did not aim to neutralize communist power with a new autocratic power but absorbed the violence of the regime, and then redirected that energy against it.

The Czech protestors of 1989 resuscitated the technique of 'political jiu-jitsu', a gentle art of subtleness, which was first popularized by Gene Sharp, an American theorist of nonviolent activism, who was influenced by the Gandhian satyagraha. Regardless of whether Havel got this tactic from Sharp or directly from the Asian martial art, or invented it on his own, he was very creative in his use of a new grammar of nonviolent politics. Havel's call to concepts such as conscience and civility attributed a more ethical foundation to the civic humanist movement of 1989. Though very European in essence, it is undeniable that the democratic movement envisaged by Havel and the members of Charter 77 was born out of a Gandhian grammar of 'ethicalization of politics'. The Velvet Revolution of 1989 embraced the Gandhian ethics of responsibility and his commitment to human dignity, while insisting on the inherent fragility of human existence and the frailty of the human political condition. Therein lies the nonviolent originality of the Velvet Revolution of 1989 and the work of its moral leaders, both in confronting the realism of political power and in speaking the truth beyond the national and the cultural frontiers by picking the right moral and political alternative.

6

The Seeds of Compassion
Mother Teresa and Dalai Lama

Tenzin Gyatso, His Holiness the Dalai Lama, the fourteenth in title, considered by his very function as a manifestation of Avalokiteshvara, 'the one who looks down, the great bodhisattva of compassion', has been the subject, like all famous figures, of numerous essays and biographical studies. Most authors present him as a saint, prophet, politician and the highest dignitary of Buddhism, but very rarely is he portrayed as a thinker of nonviolence. However, the image of His Holiness the Dalai Lama seems to have changed in recent decades. He is now considered as the true heir of Mahatma Gandhi. Indeed, since Mahatma Gandhi's death in January 1948, no one has exerted a greater influence than His Holiness the Dalai Lama on the philosophy of nonviolence, in ways different from those of a Martin Luther King, Jr., Nelson Mandela or Vaclav Havel. Though His Holiness the Dalai Lama is a practitioner of nonviolence like many of them, he also stands as a spiritual leader in the eyes of millions of Tibetans, who see him as a more perfect and accomplished being than others.

The Dalai Lama was born on 6 July 1935 in the Amdo province in northeastern Tibet. At the age of two, he was recognized by a delegation sent by the National Assembly of Lhasa as the true reincarnation of the Buddha of infinite compassion. Inducted at the age of five, Tenzin Gyatso has since been called by Tibetans 'Kundun' or 'The Presence'. Since 1959, the Dalai Lama has lived in Dharamsala, in northern India, where he leads both a spiritual and political life. Dressed in a saffron and burgundy robe, he is a man with a radiant smile and childlike laughter, who remains humble despite being presented as a living god. His Holiness is very conscious about the fact that He is not the Buddha. He proclaims,

> You know, the Buddha was a man and I am not a god. The Dalai Lama doesn't exist. It's an artificial title. If my people want me to be a head of state, I am a head of state. When in my dreams I am confronted with a problem, I always remember that I am a monk, never the Dalai Lama and even less a god.[1]

His Holiness the Dalai Lama says the same thing in his talks with Vijay Kranti: 'I think that in my subconscious the feeling of being a monk is stronger. Even in my dreams I see myself as a monk and not as a Dalai Lama who is the leader of the Tibetans.'[2] Humility seems to be an innate virtue in the Dalai Lama who presents himself, like Gandhi, as a 'seeker of truth'. This truth does not lie on the intellectual or the theoretical level, but on the level of concrete attitudes. To know it, one must follow the path of a lucid observer who lives among men and shares their miseries and problems. For Tenzin Gyatso, nonviolence is the foundation of this quest for truth. It is the only path that leads to its discovery. 'The most practical and sensible thing for all of us', writes the Dalai Lama, 'is to sit down amicably and discuss matters with respect. Reality tells us very clearly that we must come together to increase the unity of our common purpose and to exchange experiences.'[3]

The Dalai Lama considers nonviolence primarily as a mental attitude closely related to tolerance. In the field of interpersonal relations, kindness is a cardinal virtue which reflects tolerance. 'I believe', he emphasizes, 'that kindness is a great source of happiness, [for] it is impossible to achieve happiness through anger or hatred.'[4] Going further in his logic of nonviolence, he even describes kindness as the foundation of a universal religion:

> An interesting point about kindness is that one does not have to go to a temple or a monastery or sink into philosophy to practice it. The true Dharma is to think of others, not to be selfish and to worry about others. This brings people together and contributes to world peace and harmony. That is why I say that the practice of kindness is a universal religion, even for atheists and non-believers.[5]

For His Holiness, a nonviolent temperament can actively contribute to the formation of the religious spirit. Thus, every religious spirit should give priority to nonviolence as a sign of love and compassion for others, and religion has the task of forming tolerant and virtuous people. According to Tenzin Gyatso, 'any religion, any teaching, or any Dharma is intended to make good men of its followers. A good man is one who has a good heart. And the most important things for a good heart are love, compassion, tolerance and forgiveness.'[6]

The Dalai Lama's message is therefore very clear: to teach others to be good, one must be tolerant and good oneself. In other words, nonviolence awakens, according to him, the innate goodness that is inscribed in each one of us. Men are all naturally good, but they ignore their true nature, because they hide it behind the mask of violence and hatred. So His Holiness invites us to trust our nature, because it teaches us that there is

> a goodness engraved deep within us, a fundamental and all-powerful gentleness . . . . Goodness that extends to the whole universe and that will one day lead us to nirvana, but a fragile goodness, since the murder of a dog can disturb the order of the world. Secret goodness too, is easily concealed under the arrogance, brutality and greed that are the masks we most often wear.[7]

Nonviolence is, therefore, for the Dalai Lama a de facto recognition of the Other. On the one hand, it is the consolidation of something familiar and already known, which is the human goodness. On the other hand, it is a de jure recognition, which attributes to every human being the moral capacity for freedom and responsibility. As such, in His Holiness' philosophy, the basic idea of nonviolence does not merely eliminate any attitude of indifference, but it also implies a positive attitude towards others. As a matter of fact, concern for others is the foundation of universal harmony. By 'the Other' His Holiness the Dalai Lama means every living element which is part of this universal harmony. This is why he declares that 'the killing of an animal is an attack on universal harmony'.[8] This universal harmony can be summed up by the notion of 'interdependence' as taught by the Buddha. According to the teaching of the Buddha, each element in the universe is related to another, for nothing has a separate existence. There is no isolated self. Humankind is part of the universe just like any other species and must maintain its harmony through peace and compassion. Peace of mind and compassion, therefore, are indispensable qualities for the fellowship of humankind with the universe. As pointed out by His Holiness, 'Without them [peace of mind and compassion], it is useless even to try. They are indispensable, but they are also inevitable. We can reject all forms of religion, but we cannot reject compassion and peace of mind out of ourselves.'[9]

According to Tibetan Buddhism, this feeling of peace and compassion is within us, even if it is hidden and masked. No matter how restless the human spirit is with fear and hatred, this restlessness is not the dominant force. Therefore, to reach for our truth, we must respect the truth of the Other. Such a search for truth can only be based on nonviolence. As a result, since the truth sought by the Dalai Lama is the truth of both mind and action, he rejects, once and for all, the idea of doing evil in defence of any truth. This is precisely the contradiction in which certain religions find themselves, because they think that they can impose their God by violence. On this point the Dalai Lama's position is clear and unequivocal. As he observes, 'He who claims that his god is the only god commits a dangerous, harmful action, for he is on the way to imposing his belief on others by every means.'[10] It is, therefore, not necessarily faith in God that gives meaning to life, but, rather, love of humanity and of life in general that marks out the path. In fact, the love of God, which appears as the essence of different religions, is a way of accessing the truth of life, which is nonviolence. As His Holiness noted during a discussion with the Archbishop of Canterbury, 'Different beliefs are different paths leading to the same goal.'¹¹ In other words, all religions have their share of truth and their share of error. But every religious attitude must conform to the requirement of 'spiritual democracy'. This is 'the raison d'être of universal compassion. It recognizes that every living being has an equal right to happiness and the desire to be happy. It is based on the reality that the selfish needs of the individual . . . can never take precedence over the needs of the many.'¹² For the same reason, the Dalai Lama believes that every religion must submit to the will of the people, otherwise it will fail to touch the hearts of the citizens. That is why, according to His Holiness, there should be no contradiction between Buddhism and democracy. His desire for democracy for Tibet is in line with this perspective. As he observes, 'Our idea of the future of Tibet has always been very clear. Tibet should be a democracy.'¹³ As such, inventing democracy in Tibet requires the practice of nonviolence. And His Holiness adds, 'I want a free Tibet that is a zone of ahimsa and nonviolence; a sanctuary of peace where everyone can come in complete freedom to rebuild their lives.'¹⁴ One of the major concerns of His Holiness is therefore to enable Tibetans to govern themselves without resorting to the mechanisms of violent coercion. The best way to achieve this, he says, is for them to learn to practise democracy among themselves and with others. For this reason, he also sees nonviolence as the best policy. He is convinced that those who choose violence to fight the enemies of Tibet would have no choice but to govern Tibet by violence if they were to prevail. 'Some people', notes His Holiness, 'have a different point of view and think that using violence is the only way to be listened to. I admit that there is a certain logic in this way of thinking, but it is not mine. . . . For me, violence can never be the way to go.'¹⁵ We see up to what point His Holiness the Dalai Lama remains faithful to the Gandhian principle of nonviolence. Also, he never misses an opportunity to present himself as a disciple of Gandhi. 'I have faith in ahimsa', he says, 'the path of nonviolence demonstrated by Mahatma Gandhi.'[16] He returns to this subject in his interviews with Jean-Claude Carrière: 'I believe, despite certain appearances, that the notion of ahimsa, of nonviolence, scores some points. In the time of Mahatma Gandhi, a man whom I venerate, nonviolence was most often seen as weakness, as a refusal to act, almost as cowardice. That is no longer the case. The choice of non-violence is today a positive act, which evokes a strength.'[17]

In addition to Gandhi's teachings are those of the Buddha, for whom nonviolence is the very essence of religion, and who pushes respect for all living beings to the extreme. 'Our teacher', affirms the Dalai Lama, 'has shown us the path of nonviolence, tolerance and compassion.'[18] In other words, from His Holiness' point of view, Tibetans are nonviolent because they have chosen the path of Buddhism. 'All over the world', he says, 'the Tibetan people are said to be exceptionally kind and gentle. I can see only one reason for this in our culture, and that is that it has been based for centuries on the Buddhist teachings of nonviolence.'[19] These two great influences strengthen the Dalai Lama in his deep desire for peace. He considers that there can be no peace without a real practice of nonviolence, nor a nonviolent action without a real desire for peace. 'Nonviolence', he underlines, 'is the only way for the oppressed peoples of the world to move towards lasting peace.'[20] Peace is, therefore, both an internal peace and an external peace that reigns in the world. The search for the former is an indispensable key to achieving the latter.

For His Holiness the Dalai Lama, neighbourly love and the practice of nonviolence are not elitist choices, but the only choices possible in our everyday actions, because of the equivalence they establish between the ends and the means. As such, he believes that if peace and nonviolence are expressed in our everyday actions, then the challenge before us is to be able to reflect on the means. Therefore, the Dalai Lama's application of the Gandhian movement of nonviolence is also the acceptance of the fact that victory is not always immediately around the corner. What history has shown the Tibetan people is that nonviolence can be a painfully slow process. However, despite the spiritual and strategic similarities between Gandhi and the Dalai Lama, it goes without saying that there are also many differences that are quite irrefutable. According to Mayank Chhaya in his book *Dalai Lama: Man, Monk, Mystic,*

> Gandhi had the well-defined context of a country to operate in. He did not have to shoulder the burden of an ancient belief system. It was only toward the end of his life that he began to inspire an element of worship among some of his followers. Gandhi also had the support of a galaxy of powerful leaders, who were giants in their own right and helped him create perhaps the world's single biggest political movement. On Gandhi's leadership depended the destinies of over 300 million people. And most important, he was up against an imperial power in precipitous decline. The Dalai Lama, on the other hand, has no defined context of a country to operate from, although in his and other Tibetans' minds Tibet is a real geographical entity. The Dalai Lama is hamstrung by the demands of propping up an ancient belief system. He has been

worshipped since he was a child. He remains the only leader of consequence for his cause, unlike Gandhi. The future of some 6 million people rides on the Dalai Lama, although a substantial number of them have resigned themselves to their fate of being under Chinese sovereignty. And most important, he is up against a political, military, and economic power that is steeply rising.[21]

This is true, but in many ways His Holiness the Dalai Lama is the true successor of Gandhian nonviolence inasmuch as he is the last moral leader of our world. The fact that His Holiness the Dalai Lama considers the practice of nonviolence as a moral strength is in consonance with Gandhi's thought when he says,

> My nonviolence does not admit of running away from danger and leaving dear ones unprotected. Between violence and cowardly flight, I can only prefer violence to cowardice. I can no more preach non-violence to a coward than I can tempt a blind man to enjoy healthy scenes. Non-violence is the summit of bravery. And in my own experience, I have had no difficulty in demonstrating to men trained in the school of violence the superiority of non-violence. As a coward, which I was for years, I harboured violence. I began to prize non-violence only when I began to shed cowardice.[22]

In his own way, the Dalai Lama extends his belief in the moral courage of nonviolent relationship with the Other to the human ability of practising compassion. For the Dalai Lama it is thinking less about oneself and more about the others. As such, he defines nonviolence as 'compassion in action',[23] which goes to show that he considers nonviolence as an ethics of responsibility, which entails the ability to treat all beings as one. Therefore, it is the ethics of solidarity and interdependence that is stressed in the life and thought of His Holiness the Dalai Lama. The statement of the Nobel Committee for the 1989 Nobel Peace Prize expresses this clearly: 'In his efforts to promote peace the Dalai Lama has shown that what he aims to achieve is not a power base at the expense of others. He claims no more for his people than what everybody – no doubt the Chinese themselves – recognize as elementary human rights.'[24]

It would be interesting to see up to what point Mother Teresa, like His Holiness the Dalai Lama, recognized compassion as a moral force to reduce violence and replace it with nonviolence. Mother Teresa was without doubt an extraordinary spiritual character, who will remain a great apostle of nonviolence as a woman and as a nun. She dedicated her whole life to the poor and the excluded of contemporary societies, among whom she always lived. Canonized during her lifetime, she was awarded the Nobel Peace Prize in Oslo on 10 December 1979, ten years before His Holiness the Dalai Lama and fifteen years after Martin Luther King, Jr. On that day the whole world discovered a little nun wrapped in a blue and white sari, her head bowed with age, but who was humble and solemn. Since that day Mother Teresa is well known all over the world as the most important heroine of peace and nonviolence in the twentieth century. For some people she was the embodiment of the word of Christ. For others she was the symbol of empathy, solidarity and moral humanism. With her name are associated the concepts of charity, compassion and love. Following in the footsteps of the great saints of the Catholic Church, Mother Teresa shook the conscience of our world of greed and violence, projecting her nonviolent struggle against misery and exclusion onto the media stage.

Born on 26 August 1910, in Skopje, Macedonia, to Albanian parents, she chose the religious life at the age of eighteen, by deciding to enter the Sisters of Notre Dame de Loreto. As we can read in Mother Teresa's biography by Anne Sebba,

> In the two years before she decided to become a nun Agnes spent longer periods on retreat at the shrine of Cernagore and she sought guidance from her Father Confessor. He told her: 'If the thought that God may be calling you to serve him and your neighbour makes you happy, then that may be the very best proof of the genuineness of your vocation. Joy that comes from the depths of your being is like a compass by which you can tell what direction your life should follow. That is the case even when the road you must take is a difficult one.'[25]

On 25 September 1928, Agnes left through Austria, Switzerland, France and England to land in Dublin where the mother house of the congregation was located. For six weeks she learned English while preparing for her religious education. On December 2 of the same year, she left Europe to settle in India where she had her first experience of poverty. On 23 May 1929, she left for Darjeeling at the foot of the Himalayas, where she was received as a novice. In 1931, she took her first vows, taking the habit of a nun. She gave herself the name Teresa, in reference to Saint Therese of Lisieux. After a short stay in Bengal where she worked in a dispensary, she returned to Calcutta to continue her formation. Shortly afterwards, she was appointed a professor at St. Mary's College in Calcutta, where she taught more than 300 girls. But, with India's independence followed by the increasing number of refugees in Calcutta, Mother Teresa decided to leave her college and live among the poor. It was on the train that took her to Darjeeling that she heard for the first time the voice of God ordering her to leave the convent to help the poor. It was only in April 1948 that Mother Teresa received permission from the Vatican to leave the community of the Sisters of Loreto to consecrate herself to the poor. Thus, at the age of thirty-eight, she bid farewell to her habit as a nun and put on a simple white and blue sari.

Returning to Calcutta after a three-month stay in Patna with the medical mission of the 'Little Sisters of the Poor', Mother Teresa stayed at 14 Creek Street, a house which belonged to a Catholic originally from Bengal. As soon as she moved in, her former students from St. Mary's College joined her to help her in her work in the service of the poor. On 7 October 1950, she founded the Congregation of the Missionaries of Charity. The same year, she obtained Indian nationality. The statutes of the congregation were written by Fathers Julien Henri and Celest Van Exem of the Society of Jesus. To the vows of chastity, they added, at the special request of Mother Teresa, those of poverty and obedience. Over the years, the Congregation of the Missionaries of Charity grew in work and numbers. At the same time as the poor and the sick flocked in, dozens of Sisters arrived from all over the world to bring their help and their faith. Mother Teresa's first humanitarian action dates back to 1952 when she opened a store (Nirmal Hriday) in the popular district of Kalighat. It was after taking in a woman who was dying in the street that Mother Teresa decided to found this house. Navin Chawla, the Indian civil servant who became another of Teresa's biographers, notes the following: 'Mother Teresa was to tell me on several occasions, "If we did not believe that this was the body of Christ we would never be able to do this work. . . . It is Christ we touch in the broken bodies of the starving and the destitute."[26] But Mother Teresa's work didn't stop there. In the same spirit of Christian charity she also took care of lepers and, with the help of the Indian government and the people of Calcutta, founded the 'Shanti Nagar' (City of Peace), which later became a rehabilitation centre for lepers. Her motto was: Leprosy is not a punishment, it can be a very beautiful gift of God if we make good use of it. Through it, we can learn to love the unloved, the unwanted; not only just to give them things but to make them feel that they, too, are useful, that they too can do something because they feel they are loved and wanted that they can share the joy of living.[27]

After going to Amman, Guatemala and Beirut, Mother Teresa decided to work for AIDS patients. She met with heads of state from around the world to ask them to help her in her work. The Pope offered her a home inside Vatican City to help the excluded. In April 1990, she decided to entrust the leadership of her congregation to someone younger, but she was re-elected by the other nuns. It was only in 1996, a year before her death that she resigned for health reasons and was replaced by Sister Nirmala. Until the last days of her life, she continued to devote herself fully and passionately to the poor and the excluded, as well as to peace and nonviolence in the world. In a letter to George Bush and Saddam Hussein in January 1991, she wrote:

I come to you with tears in my eyes and God's love in my heart to plead to you for the poor and those who will become poor if the war that we all dread and fear happens. I beg you with my whole heart to work for, to labour for God's peace and to be reconciled with one another. . . . In the short term there may be winners and losers in this war that we all dread, but that never can, nor never will justify the suffering, pain and loss of life which your weapons will cause. . . . I appeal to you – to your love, your love of God and your fellow men. In the name of God and in the name of those you will make poor, do not destroy life and peace. Let love and peace triumph and let your names be remembered for the good you have done, the joy you have spread and the love you have shared.[28]

A heroine of nonviolence, Mother Teresa was also a woman of compassion. That is why, it is necessary to be attentive to the vocabulary she used. She constantly qualified her Christian action, in the face of the harsh reality with which she was confronted, with words charged with compassionate weight such as charity or love, terms that must be situated in relation to her spiritual attitude. Far from doing only the work of a social worker, she was looking for a new mode of thinking and a new way of living which found its roots in the figure of Christ. For Mother Teresa it is this figure of Christ which expresses what this love can be, which is not possession, but a gift. It is a direct love: it goes from one heart to another; but it is also a love-action: it creates a commitment and a responsibility towards the other. In this way Mother Teresa rediscovered the spirit of the first Church, and joined the spirit of Christian mystics like St. Francis of Assisi, who believed that the only possible way to attest to the faith was to pay great attention to the problems of this world. Mother Teresa never spoke, or spoke very little, of justice and nonviolence, yet she defended the very idea of justice through her nonviolent action. For her, injustice could be summed up in two things: the rejection of the Other and the lack of love for the Other.

Though Mother Teresa's nonviolent stance was not a device for immediate conflict resolution or social protest, it was, nonetheless, a compassionate ethics for universal responsibility and a powerful plea for tolerance. In this sense, it would be wrong to consider Mother Teresa and her charitable work as a Christian nun outside the Gandhian movement for social change. If that is the case, then it can be said that Mother Teresa, like Mahatma Gandhi, Martin Luther King, Jr., Nelson Mandela, Vaclav Havel and His Holiness the Dalai Lama, was a practitioner of nonviolence who showed us a new way to the world and to the Otherness of the Other. Mother Teresa's famous motto was: 'We are all called to love, love until it hurts.'[29] When saying this she was trying not only to express her love for her fellow human beings, but also to make us conscious about the power of love as a force of change in the world. In the manner of Mahatma Gandhi and Martin Luther King, Jr., Mother Teresa projected the ethic of love to the centre of our lives. In 1967, addressing a group of anti-war clergymen, Martin Luther King, Jr. observed: 'When I speak of love, I am not speaking of some sentimental and weak response. I am speaking of that force which all of the great religions have seen as the supreme unifying principle of life. Love is somehow the key that unlocks the door which leads to ultimate reality.'[30] Though not a theorist of nonviolence, Mother Teresa knew well that at the centre of any nonviolent action, taking into consideration the otherness of the Other, stands the principle of love. But this call for universal fellowship and cosmic companionship could not happen without a true revolution of values. King in his own way and with his own personal approach to Christianity defined this revolution of values in the following terms:

> A true revolution of values will soon cause us to question the fairness and justice of many of our past and present policies. On the one hand we are called to play the good Samaritan on life's roadside; but that will be only an initial act. One day we must come to see that the whole Jericho road must be transformed so that men and women will not be constantly beaten and robbed as they make their journey on life's highway. True compassion is more than flinging a coin to a beggar. It comes to see that an edifice which produces beggars needs restructuring.[31]

Most of the practitioners of nonviolence, those dissenter gadflies like Gandhi and King, or empathetic civic leaders like Mandela and Havel, or compassionate apostles of love like His Holiness the Dalai Lama and Mother Teresa, knew well that one day their ethic of nonviolence and their strength of compassion, civility and reconciliation would bring their dreams to fruition and nonviolent resistance to fulfilment. So we come full circle. The struggle for love, truth, justice and nonviolence has also been a lifelong effort for humanity to overcome her own evils. Evils so crystal clear and self-evident, like racism, anti-Semitism, homophobia, religious fundamentalism, militarism, etc., that they have imprisoned us in mental ghettos of intolerance, hatred and violence. Alas, our civilization continues to produce violence and to worship it as a mode of living and resisting. But while humanity continues to suffer in its meaningless violence and tragic absurdity, a creative synthesis of dissent and empathy can lead us through the dark valleys of our world and into pathways of nonviolence. Would this be a utopian dream or a process of waiting for a messiah? Surely not, but maybe at times we need to understand that the acceptance of empathy and welcoming of nonviolence can threaten the basic values of our world by leading us away from our mental zones of comfort and make us come to terms with our evils in the face of our great civilizational losses.

Conclusion
Limits of Nonviolence

In a little town in Poland, the Jewish community hired a man to sit outside the entrance to the town to watch for the messiah, so that when the messiah was on his way, this guy could tell the Jews in the town to get ready. And somebody said to him, 'This is a job? You're sitting and watching for the messiah?' He said, 'Yes, it's a job – the pay isn't so good, but it's steady work.' Nonviolence is certainly not a job, but it is steady work. Perhaps since the dawn of civilization, nonviolence has been considered as a noble ideal, but many believed that violence is the best way to get immediate results. It is true that nonviolence, by definition, cannot be acquired in a day. Nonviolence demands a time of patience and a moral preparation. There is no half-way between the ethical and the nonviolent on the one hand, and the unethical and the violent, on the other. As Gandhi says,

We may never be strong enough to be entirely nonviolent in thought, word and deed. But we must keep nonviolence as our goal and make steady progress towards it. The attainment of freedom, whether for a man, a nation or the world, must be in exact proportion to the attainment of nonviolence by each. Let those, therefore, who believe in nonviolence as the only method of achieving real freedom keep the lamp of nonviolence burning bright in the midst of the present impenetrable gloom. The truth of a few will count; the untruth of millions will vanish even like chaff before whiff of wind.[1]

What history shows us is that the struggle against inequality, injustice and authoritarianism requires moments of popular mobilization, civil society empowerment and insurgency. These are moments when social ills and political evils are challenged by a kind of eruption of dissent and moral resistance. We often use the term 'nonviolent revolution' to explain social and political changes that use nonviolent tactics and strategies in order to bring about the departure of governments seen as illiberal, authoritarian and repressive. But it would be more appropriate to use the term 'nonviolent resistance'. Moreover, when one resists, one is taking a stand against something. But to resist in a nonviolent way is to take a stand against a violent act and to react at the same time against a situation which has become intolerable. However, any form of resistance is at the same time a form of dissidence and disobedience. In a deeper sense, the democratic citizen owes his final allegiance to his own capacity of self-government and to his democratic courage and constitutional necessity to disobey unjust laws. As such, dissent and disobedience are justified both morally and politically because of the closure of political processes in the public sphere. And here, we can add immediately that the appeal to social stability as an argument against the moral and political obligations to disobey cannot be used to condemn the act of questioning and disobeying as a mode of exit from self-incurred immaturity and infantilism. Actually, when we equate nonviolent disobedience with chaos or instability, we seem to

envision a society in which civil disobedience is a general refusal of
the essence of the law. But the point is that civil disobedience not
only does have a great intrinsic worth, but it is also a means towards a
democratic end. The key point here is that the institutionalization of
civil disobedience as an act of dissent not only educates the citizens
and increases their opportunities to participate in the public realm,
but also helps the process of democratizing democracies. Tolstoy
considered civil disobedience as a spiritual strategy that could break
the vicious circle of social and political violence. He had a firm belief
that the most tyrannical and despotic regime may be contained by
nonviolent civil disobedience, which he described as non-payment of
taxes, non-obeying of laws and giving up every sort of governmental
service. Tolstoy's ideas have a great resemblance to those of Henry
David Thoreau, who was immortalized by his essay 'On the Duty of
Civil Disobedience' and his refusal to pay his taxes in order not to
provide material support to a federal government that perpetuated
mass injustice – in particular, slavery and the Mexican–American
war. The same views were later adopted by Martin Luther King, Jr.
However, the immediate practical successor of Tolstoy and Thoreau
was Gandhi, who in his autobiography, 'My Experiments with Truth',
declared himself a humble disciple of Tolstoy and an avid reader of
Thoreau. Like Thoreau, Gandhi believed that the individual is the
higher and independent power from which all of the government's
own power and authority are derived. That is why, according to
Gandhi, it is the government which should have the sanction of the
governed. The point taken by Gandhi from Thoreau, and later fully
developed by Martin Luther King, is that one's inner sense of justice
is above the laws. This invokes the concept of responsibility against

the idea of obedience. For King, the ethical foundation of disobeying the law is also the ethical imperative of the universe. That is why, according to him, the person who disobeys and accepts to suffer for its consequences does not make others suffer by his or her own defiance of the law. In other words, for King, living with nonviolence is an attempt to regain control over one's own sense of life. So, as in the case of Gandhi, with King we have continuity between the obligation to disobey and the spiritual transformation of the individual. In that case, nonviolent disobedience, as a form of nonviolent civility, creates the change in values both in the individual and in the institutions of civil society. Maybe that is why nonviolence is the way in which our dissident mind can be exercised in its entirety.

Dissidence is not necessarily a political act, but it could be an intellectual state of mind. But when we talk about a dissident, as was the case with Andrei Sakharov in Soviet Union or Vaclav Havel in ex-Czechoslovakia, we mean essentially a person who formally opposes the policies of a current political structure. Accordingly, in ex-Communist regimes, the term 'dissident' came to refer to individuals who 'sat apart' from the political establishment and were nonconformists. A dissident is a person with a dissenting mind, who would not agree with something that other people agree with. The word 'dissent' derives from the Latin *dissentire*, which means 'to feel apart'. But the term also describes a situation of disagreement and contradiction. In that case, dissent is a public act of disagreement with the ideas, doctrines or decrees of an establishment, be it a political party, a government or the official representatives of a religion. The complexity of 'dissent' emerges when we refer to 'dissidence' as being nonconformist by nature. A nonconformist is someone who lives and thinks in a way that is different from other individuals and who does not conform to a generally accepted pattern of thought. But what makes some individuals nonconformist? Is it only for the sake of being different? Actually, a nonconformist is someone who has the desire to excel. To excel is to surpass others in accomplishment or achievement in order to distinguish oneself. In other words, to be a dissident is to have the quality of excellence. For the ancient Greeks, excellence was considered as a moral virtue. As such, the Greeks saw it as bound up with the act of living up to one's full potential. This passion for excellence and moral greatness was aroused among Greek philosophers like Socrates. For Socrates, dissidence was an exemplary act of excellence. To understand Socrates truly as a practitioner of nonviolence, we need to consider the Socratic legacy of dissent and critical public questioning as an expression of nonviolent marginality. The Socratic act of questioning is different from the everyday habitual practices of asking questions, if any questions are asked. It is the exercise of a nonviolent dissident mind. As a dissident mind, Socrates brought about a revaluation of the values of his time. By bringing the philosophical revolt into Athens, Socrates not only threatened the priority of the polis, but he also subordinated politics to the ethical content of philosophical interrogation. Maybe that is why since Socrates, nonviolent dissent and disobedience has been the most valuable safeguard of democracy. Over the centuries, this Socratic moment of nonviolent dissent has been acknowledged and endorsed by all practitioners of nonviolence as an ethical horizon of responsibility without which life in common has no meaning. That is why, any democratic society that turns into a consumer value system and creates no sense of responsibility higher than the simple ideals of a political party or a multinational corporation will end up becoming a community of mediocrity.

Frankly speaking, it is not because we think and act democratically that we create good democratic institutions. What makes a democracy democratic is its dissenting force of transvaluing its values. A dissenting society should require its citizens to struggle for the moral progress of their community. As such, the goal of a democratic society is not only to defend individual rights inscribed in a constitution, but also to be able to give birth to a new generation of citizens who understand and underline the value of rights. But we will never be able to preserve our democracies, if we do not at the same time promote a culture of nonviolence and encourage the philosophical and political imperatives of doubting and questioning. What is being said here is that nonviolent resistance has the political capacity to re-energize democratic citizenship and free it from conformity, complacency and corruption. That is why nonviolence is our passport to the future, for tomorrow belongs to the people who will learn how to live together in peace without degrading and destroying each other. Truly, violence is one of the worst failures of humanity, which continues to put our individual and social lives in danger in the third decade of the twenty-first century. What is to be done? Peoples and politicians around the world seem to be deaf and blind to the humanist legacy of nonviolent practitioners like Gandhi, Martin Luther King, Jr., Mandela and others. But despite this forgetfulness, our recent history shows us that each time we tried to find ethical and political ways to oppose violence, humanity has given the culture of peace a solid foundation on which to build an active openness to difference, with genuine intercultural dialogue. This is the milestone to be crossed in order to make it possible to establish within a community and between communities, a framework of peaceful coexistence. How do we do that? By a revolution of values, or in other terms, by a radical reversal of attitudes. This power to change attitudes and values puts any form of nonviolent dissidence and dissent in illegality and on the side of the revolutionary spirit. However, we can say that nonviolent dissent, despite its radicality, is compatible with the spirit of democracy. If we agree that 'consent' is the outcome of a social contract, and that a democratic contract is the rule of a representative or direct democracy over willing subjects who have the potential and the possibility to change the rulers, then consent is not a vertical phenomenon, but a horizontal one. However, consent can be valid if and only if dissent is considered as a democratic act and de facto possibility for citizens to change the norms and the institutions. This brings us back to the relation between nonviolence and freedom in a society. If the essence of freedom is the dynamic of entering the public world and adding something new to it, then the preservation of freedom is deeply grounded in the act of nonviolent resistance. In reality, nonviolent resistance is a determined mind operating in a political world in some respects indeterminate, because it is open ended and moving towards a new future. Nonviolent resistance is a privileged moment of an ethical revolt against cynicism, mediocrity and violence, which requires trust in the goodness of humankind. It, therefore, involves civic education, and a balance between ethics and politics. This is the way that was always taken by the champions of nonviolence. They never sacrificed the ideal of a radical change in the mentalities of the citizens and the hierarchical structures of the societies that animated them.

It is through the spirit of this nobility that we must try to make nonviolence effective everywhere. If we are convinced that there is a positive value of nonviolence for the future of humanity, then there are historical forms of nonviolence that are quite valid for our twenty-first century and beyond. Nonviolence is therefore not a new idea. It is as old as the history of humankind. One only needs to look at how the constant rejection of the legitimization of violence was thought and elaborated wherever tyrannies, prejudices and intolerances were perpetuated. The illegitimacy of violence has always gone hand in hand with the legitimacy of the otherness of the Other. As Thomas Merton remarks majestically, 'The nonviolent resister is not fighting simply for "his" truth or for "his" pure conscience, or for the right that is on "his side". On the contrary, both his strength and his weakness come from the fact that he is fighting for the truth, common to him and to the adversary, the right which is objective and universal. He is fighting for everybody.'[2] This 'common moral horizon' in the process of nonviolent resistance is an understanding that nonviolence is a form of political association that can accommodate the plurality of opinions. But it is also a dialogical conception of citizenship, which listens to the other with empathy, while hoping for a minimal decent society. But the big question would be whether there is any way to build a nonviolent society in a world of fanaticism and sectarianism that renounces recognition of others. This question is followed by a second one: Why is this departure from tolerance happening in a world that flatters itself for being a village of multiculturalism and global integration? Why this increasing division of our common house into fundamentalist camps shouting and killing each other? Does this mean that there are limits to the human mental and physical capacities to be nonviolent? If that was the case, we would not have witnessed an intensification of nonviolent protests in the past few years around the globe. Protests in Iran, Hong Kong, Chile, Beirut, Venezuela, France and so on are powerful reminders of Gandhi's enduring political relevance and a pioneering account of his extraordinary intellectual achievements. Today, nonviolence in international politics is a matter of nonviolent organization of the world bringing peace and interconnectedness among cultures and civilizations. As mentioned previously, Gandhian nonviolence has been instrumental in political transitions from authoritarian or oppressive rule for many decades. Indeed, nonviolent revolutions, characterized by civil society organization, mass mobilization and negotiation have revolutionized the very concept of revolution. Long gone are the days when the very concept of revolution was synonymous with state capture or overthrow through guerilla warfare or Leninist vanguard activism.

Today, nonviolence is a cry of humanity in the face of barbarism. To be anti-barbarian in our time is to say 'no' unconditionally to violence. Finding a common ground can work only if we share enough to behave civilly. But fanatics and fundamentalists always reject civility and compassion, because they believe that they have the absolute truth and end up denying other people's existence. If fundamentalism, in all its different forms, is akin to violence in its mode of thinking and its methods of acting, it cannot expect to be recognized or tolerated by others. This is what creates the cycle of violence. One who steps on people will get stepped on by the people. But as we see in the multiple examples of the practice of nonviolence in India, America, South Africa and Central Europe, nonviolence and reconciliation are possible even if atrocities are committed by the previous regimes. As history shows us, sometimes human beings can surprise us. Sometimes they have a great capacity for compassion and forgiveness, but they also hold an ability for seeking truth and justice. In that case, they would have faith in nonviolence and they will act nonviolently. This is possible only if people see themselves as neither victims nor executioners. We need to go back and read again the brilliant essay by Albert Camus entitled, 'Neither Victims nor Executioners' as a forceful response to those who justify murder and violence. Camus observes,

> All I ask is that, in the midst of a murderous world, we agree to reflect on murder and to make a choice. After that, we can distinguish those who accept the consequences of being murderers themselves or the accomplices of murderers, and those who refuse to do so with all their force and being. Since this terrible dividing line does actually exist, it will be a gain if it be clearly marked. Over the expanse of five continents throughout the coming years an endless struggle is going to be pursued between violence and friendly persuasion, a struggle in which, granted, the former has a thousand times the chances of success than that of the latter. But I have always held that, if he who bases his hopes on human nature is a fool, he who gives up in the face of circumstances is a coward. And henceforth, the only honorable course will be to stake everything on a formidable gamble: that words are more powerful than munitions.[3]

It is difficult enough to continue reposing faith in the human capacity for self-restraint and self-transformation, but to plead for nonviolence and to endeavour to practise it, going beyond the spirit of revenge and retribution so prevalent in our own imperfect time, is a Herculean challenge that cannot be taken lightly. Our present world suffers from an arrogant superficiality that seems to be not only a form of thoughtlessness but also a total disbelief in the great moral achievements of prophets of nonviolence like Gandhi and King. Frankly, despite the symbolic devotion shown to Gandhi by politicians in India and around the world, there is a feeling of comfort that a stubborn and critical veteran of democratic action like him is not around anymore. But what if Gandhi and King were alive? They would have certainly tried to create awareness in the minds of the younger generation. Let us also agree that someone like Gandhi would have had a strong intervention (for example, fasting unto death) in relation to the cases of corruption and populist demagogy in everyday politics. How do we approach nonviolence and the art of dissent in our everyday life? Do we teach our conformist and complacent citizens to develop the habit of questioning the reality of the world without necessarily taking it for granted? In every society, Western or Eastern, modern or traditional, the major thrust of socialization is always to encourage a strong sense of obedience to the existing social norms, value systems and institutions. Nonviolent dissent is hardly encouraged; rather, the dissenter is punished. Actually, the core idea of the philosophy of nonviolent resistance is to extend our nonviolent disobedience to people in power by testing the viability of their authority or actions on moral and ethical grounds. The Gandhian moment of dissent is especially valuable in our troubled times. It can lead to courage and questioning which can earn freedom and justice. Returning to Gandhian nonviolence is a serious and conscientious commitment to explore new vistas of sociopolitical and economic transformations for our World House, at a time when populism and mass immaturity are holding each other in sway. As such, nonviolence as a spirit and as an act has an ethical significance more than just a tactical value in today's struggle for freedom and justice. As populism and authoritarianism enter democracies from the backdoor, nonviolent dissent holds out as the last bastion of citizen vigilantism against injustice. Let us not forget that it takes very little for a democracy to slip into the authoritarian mode. Therefore, the ultimate allegiance of citizens is towards the rejection of what cannot be questioned and is not accountable. As we made it clear throughout this work, nonviolent resistance stems from a philosophy of compassion, responsibility and dissent. While there are limits to nonviolent resistance and no one could advocate total nonviolence, it goes without saying that no form of self-defence against violence can justify murder. As a result, nonviolent resistance leaves room for a philosophy which recognizes the value of human life and the perpetual struggle against murder. This critique of murder takes shape in the encounter of every subject with the otherness of the Other. Thus, the acknowledgement of the Other is actually accompanied by an awareness of one's fallibility and the impossibility to maintain oneself unflinchingly in an unquestionable and unaccountable ideological stance without being in dialogue with the world. Therefore, the ethical and dialogical elements at the heart of the philosophy of nonviolent resistance remind us that a non-solidaristic self who forsakes his or her empathy and compassion for the primacy of a selfish and self-centred self cannot cherish the idea of the moral progress of humanity. Last but not least, in reassessing the struggle for the otherness of the Other, the philosophy of nonviolence can help us see the way towards a democratic form of intersubjectivity. Therefore, the larger problem is not how to choose between the realism of politics and the idealism of ethics, but how to restore the Gandhian project of ethical responsibility and nonviolent engagement in today's world. In this sense, the frailty of humankind to commit violence does not necessarily mean that it should conform to the fatality of history. What the history of nonviolence shows us is that the evils that humankind brings down upon itself are not unavoidable. In the last analysis, we can say that the Gandhian legacy of compassionate justice and empathetic solidarity can be an effort towards the making of a better world.

NOTES

Introduction

1 Mohandas Karamchand Gandhi, *My Nonviolence* (Ahmedabad: Navajivan Publishing House, 1960), pp. 49–50.

2 Ibid., p. 114.

3 Henry David Thoreau, 'Resistance to Civil Government', in *The Higher Law: Thoreau on Civil Disobedience and Reform* (Princeton: Princeton University Press, 1973), p. 63.

4 Mohandas Karamchand Gandhi, *Harijan*, November 1, 1936, p. 380, in *Collected Works of Mahatma Gandhi* (New Delhi: Publications Division Government of India, 1999), vol. 62, p. 92.

5 Leo Tolstoy, 'The Kingdom of God Is within You', in *The Kingdom of God and Peace Essays*, trans. Aylmer Maude (New Delhi: Rupa, 2001), p. 265.

6 Granville Austin, *The Indian Constitution: Cornerstone of a Nation* (Delhi: Oxford University Press, 1966), p. 31.

7 Hannah Arendt, *The Promise of Politics* (New York: Schocken Books, 2005), pp. 128–9.

8 Hannah Arendt, *On Violence* (New York: Harcourt Brace& Company, 1970), p. 53.

9 Ibid., p. 35.

10 Ibid., p. 44.

11 Ibid., p. 53.

12 Richard J. Bernstein, *Violence: Thinking without Banisters* (Cambridge: Polity, 2013), p. 88.

13 Ibid., p. 182.

14 Hannah Arendt, *On Revolution* (Harmondsworth: Penguin, 1990 [1963]), pp. 86–7.

15 Gene Sharp, 'Gandhi's Answer: Neither Peace Nor War but Nonviolent Struggle', in Anand Sharma (ed.), *Gandhian Way: Peace, Nonviolence and Empowerment* (New Delhi: Academic Foundation, 2007), p. 81.

16 Mohandas Karamchand Gandhi, 'Young India, June 30, 1920', quoted in Nirmal Kumar Bose, *Selections from Gandhi* (Ahmedabad Navajivan, 1948), p. 116.

17 Mohandas Karamchand Gandhi, *Young India, June 1, 1921*.

18 Martin Luther King Jr., *The Trumpet of Conscience* (New York: Harper & Row Publishers, Inc., 1968), p. 69.

19 Mohandas Karamchand Gandhi, 'Young India, 5-11-1931', in Krishna Kripalani (ed.), *All Men are Brothers*, (New York: Continuum, 1980), p. 118.

20 Martin Luther King, *A Testament of Hope: The Essential Writings of Martin Luther King, Jr.*, ed. James Melvin Washington (New York: Harper & Row, 1986), p. 9.

21 Ibid., p. 349.

22 Ibid., p. 18.

Chapter 1

1 Bernstein, *Violence*, p. 6.

2 See David Caute, *Fanon* (London: Fontana/ Collins, 1970), p. 81.

3 Emmanuel Hansen, *Frantz Fanon: Social and Political Thought* (Ohio: Ohio University Press, 1977), pp. 127–8.

4 Ibid., pp. 8, 126.

5 Frantz Fanon, *The Wretched of the Earth* (New York: Grove Press, 1963), p. 96.

6 Emmanuel B. Eyo and Amambo Edung Essien, 'Frantz Fanon's Philosophy of Violence and the Participation of Intellectuals in the Advancement of Social Liberation in Africa', *Africology: The Journal of Pan African Studies* 10, no. 3 (May 2017): 67.

7 Arendt, *On Violence*, pp. 65–6.

8 Bernstein, *Violence,* p. 118.

9 Coretta Scott King, *The Words of Martin Luther King, Jr.* (New York: Newmarket Press, 1987), pp. 58–9.

10 Hannah Arendt, *Between Past and Future* (New York: Penguin Books, 1993), p. 279.

11 Martin Luther King, *Where Do We Go From Here: Chaos or Community?* (Boston: Beacon Press, 2010), p. 191.

12 Albert Camus, *Resistance, Rebellion and Death*, trans. Justin O'Brien (New York: Vintage, 1995), p. 28.

13 Albert Camus, *Essais* (Paris: Gallimard, La Pleiade, 1965), pp. 355–6, quoted in John Foley, *Albert Camus: From the Absurd to Revolt* (Stocksfield: Acumen, 2008), p. 97.

14 Jean-Paul Sartre, Preface to Franz Fanon, *The Wretched of the Earth*, p. lv.

15 Victoria Tahmasebi-Birgani, *Emmanuel Levinas and the Politics of Nonviolence* (Toronto: University of Toronto Press, 2014), p. 7.

16 Emmanuel Levinas, *Totality and Infinity*, trans. Alphonso Lingis (The Hague: Martinus Nijhoff, 1969), p. 84.

17 Tahmasebi-Birgani, *Emmanuel Levinas and the Politics of Nonviolence*, p. 161.

18 Predrag Cicovacki (ed.), *The Ethics of Nonviolence: Essays by Robert L. Holmes* (New York: Bloomsbury, 2013), pp. 163–4.

19 Adorno, cited in John Sanbonmatsu, 'Introduction', in John Sanbonmatsu (ed.), *Critical Theory and Animal Liberation* (Lanham: Rowman & Littlefield, 2011), p. 10.

20 Thoreau, 'Resistance to Civil Government', p. 65.

21 Albert Einstein, *Ideas and Opinions* (New York: Crown Publishers, 1954), p. 111.

Chapter 2

1 Ramachandra Guha, *Gandhi Before India* (New York: Random House, 2014), p. 247.

2 Anthony J. Parel (ed.), *Gandhi: Hind Swaraj and Other Writings* (Cambridge: Cambridge University Press, 1997), p. 6.

3 Ibid., p. lviii.

4 King, *Testament of Hope*, p. 429.

5 Howard Zinn, Introduction to Henry David Thoreau, *The Higher Law: Thoreau on Civil Disobedience and Reform* (Princeton: Princeton University Press, 1973), p. xxi.

6 Henry David Thoreau, *The Higher Law: Thoreau on Civil Disobedience and Reform* (Princeton: Princeton University Press, 1973), p. 104.

7 Ibid., p. 98.

8 Len Gougeon, 'Thoreau and Reform', in Joel Myerson (ed.), *The Cambridge Companion to Henry David Thoreau* (Cambridge: Cambridge University Press, 1995), p. 202.

9 Ibid., p. 66.

10 Ibid., p. 179.

11 Ibid., p. 87.

12 Ralph Waldo Emerson, 'Thoreau', in Walter Harding (ed.), *Thoreau: A Century of Criticism* (Dallas: Southern Methodist University Press, 1965), pp. 26, 40.

13 Alan D. Hodder, 'The Religious Horizon', in James S. Finley (ed.), *Henry David Thoreau in Context* (Cambridge: Cambridge University Press, 2017), pp. 86–7.

14 Thoreau, *The Higher Law*, pp. 133, 134.

15 Ibid., p. 170.

16 Richard J. Schneider, 'Walden', in Myerson (ed.), *The Cambridge Companion to Henry David Thoreau*, p. 103.

17 Daniel S. Malachuk, 'Politics', in James S. Finley (ed.), *Henry David Thoreau in Context* (Cambridge: Cambridge University Press, 2017), p. 177.

18 Walter Harding, *The Days of Henry Thoreau: A Biography* (New York: Alfred Knopf, 1967), p. 207.

19 Thoreau, *The Higher Law*, p. 65.

20 Ibid., pp. 72–3.

21 Sophocles, *The Three Theban Plays* (New York: Penguin Books, 1982), p. 82.

22 Quoted in Walter Harding, *A Thoreau Handbook* (New York: New York University Press, 1959), p. 201.

23 Henry David Thoreau, *Walden* (Toronto: Ryerson Press, 1965), p. 155.

24 Mahatma Gandhi, *The Essential Writings* (Oxford: Oxford University Press, 2008), p. 359.

Chapter 3

1 Mahatma Gandhi, *Collected Works of Mahatma Gandhi* (New Delhi: Publications Division, Government of India, 1999), vol. 70, p. 296.

2 Gandhi, *Essential Writings*, p. 56.

3 Rajmohan Gandhi, *Mohandas: A True Story of a Man, His People and an Empire* (New Delhi: Penguin-Viking, 2006), p. 124.

4 Guha, *Gandhi Before India*, p. 9.

5 Quoted in Martin Green, *Tolstoy and Gandhi, Men of Peace* (New York: Basic Books, 1983), p. 97.

6 Quoted in Parel, *Gandhi: Hind Swaraj and Other Writings*, p. 136.

7 Quoted in Raghavan Iyer (ed.), *The Moral and Political Writings of Mahatma Gandhi* (Oxford: Clarendon Press, 1986), vol. II, p. 237.

8 Bhikhu Parekh, *Colonialism, Tradition and Reform* (New Delhi: Sage publications, 1999), p. 129.

9 Ibid., p. 148.

10 Ibid., p. 84.

11 George Woodcock, *Gandhi* (London: Fontana, 1972), p. 14.

12 Ibid., p. 56.

13 Parel, *Gandhi: Hind Swaraj and Other Writings*, pp. 50–1.

14 Anthony J. Parel and Judith M. Brown, *The Cambridge Companion to Gandhi* (Cambridge: Cambridge University Press, 2011), p. 170.

15 Mahatma Gandhi, *Young India*, 5 January 1922, quoted in Parel and Brown, *The Cambridge Companion to Gandhi*, p. 121.

16 Ibid., p. 123.

17 Quoted in Iyer, *The Moral and Political Writings of Mahatma Gandhi*, vol. 1, p. 116.

18　Quoted in N. K. Bose, *Selections from Gandhi* (Ahmedabad: Navajivan Publishing House, 1968), p. 37.

19　Anthony J. Parel, *Gandhi's Philosophy and the Quest for Harmony* (Cambridge: Cambridge University Press, 2006), p. 196.

20　Quoted in David Hardiman, *Gandhi in His Time and Ours* (New York: Columbia University Press, 2003), p. 53.

21　Mohandas K. Gandhi, *Harijan*, 1 June 1940, in *Non-Violent Resistance (Satyagraha)* (New York: Dover Publications, 1961), p. 307.

22　Gandhi, *Collected Works of Mahatma Gandhi*, vol. 72, p. 416.

23　Ibid., vol. 8, p. 229.

24　Woodcock, *Gandhi*, p. 96.

25　Quoted in Francis G. Hutchins, *India's Revolution: Gandhi and the Quit India Movement* (Cambridge, MA: Harvard University Press, 1973), p. 201.

Chapter 4

1　King, *A Testament of Hope*, pp. 266-7.

2　Kenneth L. Smith and Ira G. Zepp, *Search for the Beloved Community: The Thinking of Martin Luther King, Jr.* (Valley Forge: Judson Press, 1974), p. 48.

3　Ibid., p. 54.

4　Quoted in King, *A Testament of Hope*, p. 293.

5　Ibid., p. 293.

6　Ibid., p. 12.

7　Ibid., pp. 297-8.

8　Quoted in Stephen B. Oates, *Let the Trumpet Sound* (New York: Harper, 1982), pp. 81-2.

9　Smith and Zepp, *Search for the Beloved Community*, pp. 54-5.

10　Quoted in Oates, *Let the Trumpet Sound*, p. 153.

11　Ibid., pp. 77-8.

12 King, *A Testament of Hope*, p. 52.

13 Ibid., pp. 8–9.

14 Smith and Zepp, *Search for the Beloved Community*, p. 64.

15 Ibid., p. 122.

16 King, *A Testament of Hope*, p. 40.

17 Martin Luther King, Jr., *Where Do We Go From Here: Chaos or Community?* (New York: Harper & Row, 1967), p. 181.

18 King, *A Testament of Hope*, pp. 317–18.

19 Ibid., pp. 236–7.

20 Martin Luther King, *Where Do We Go From Here: Chaos or Community?* (Boston: Beacon Press, 1986), p. 181.

21 Ibid., p. 66.

22 Ibid., p. 190.

23 Clayborne Carson, *The Autobiography of Martin Luther King, Jr.* (New York: Grand Central Publishing, 2001), p. 340.

24 Martin Luther King, Jr., *Strength to Love* (New York: Harper& Row, 1963), p. 64.

25 King, *A Testament of Hope*, p. 87.

26 Desmond Tutu, *No Future Without Forgiveness* (New York: DoubleDay, 1999), p. 280.

Chapter 5

1 Quoted in Tom Lodge, *Mandela: A Critical Life* (Oxford: Oxford University Press, 2006), p. 201.

2 Nelson Mandela, *Long Walk to Freedom* (London: Abacus, 1994), p. 13.

3 Ibid., p. 110.

4 Nelson Mandela, *Conversations with Myself* (Auckland: DoubleDay, 2010), p. 45.

5 Mandela, *Long Walk to Freedom*, p. 433.

6 Quoted in Lodge, *Mandela: A Critical Life*, p. 91.

7 Nelson Mandela, 'National Liberation', quoted in Philip Bonner, 'The Antinomies of Nelson Mandela', in Rita Barnard, *The Cambridge Companion to Nelson Mandela* (Cambridge: Cambridge University Press, 2014), p. 45.

8 Jonathan Hyslop, 'Mandela and War', in Barnard, *Cambridge Companion to Nelson Mandela*, p. 163.

9 Ibid., p. 164.

10 Mandela, *Conversations with Myself*, pp. 52–3.

11 Peter Hain, *Mandela: His Essential Life* (London: Rowman & Littlefield, 2018), p. 78.

12 Lodge, *Mandela: A Critical Life*, p. 91.

13 Quoted in Hain, *Mandela: His Essential Life,* p. 149.

14 Sifiso M. Ndlovu, 'Mandela's Presidential Years: An Africanist View', in Barnard, *Cambridge Companion to Nelson Mandela*, p. 193.

15 Michael Žantovský, *Havel: A Life* (London: Atlantic Books, 2016), pp. 199–200.

16 Ibid.

17 Vaclav Havel, 'The Power of the Powerless', in John Keane (ed.), *The Power of the Powerless: Citizens Against the State in Central-Eastern Europe* (London: Routledge, 1985), p. 51.

18 Ibid., p. 43.

19 Gandhi, *All Men Are Brothers* (Ahmedabad: Navajivan Publishing, 1971), pp. 144–5.

20 Žantovský, *Havel: A Life*, p. 238.

21 Vaclav Havel, *Summer Meditations* (New York: Vintage Books, 1993), pp. 100–1.

22 Ibid., p. 18.

23 Žantovský, *Havel: A Life*, p. 385.

24 Vaclav Havel, *Disturbing the Peace: A Conversation with Karel Hvížďala* (New York: Alfred A. Knopf, 1990), p. 190.

25 Havel, *Summer Meditations*, p. 6.

26 Žantovský, *Havel: A Life*, pp. 201, 437.

27 Havel, *Summer Meditations*, pp. 129–30.

28 Quoted in Amir Weiner and John Connelly, *Contemporary European History*, vol. 18, no. 3, 'Revisiting 1989: Causes, Course and Consequences' (August 2009), p. 247.

Chapter 6

1 Claudine, Vernier Palliez and Auger Benjamin, *Le Dalai Lama - La Presence Et L'exil* (Paris: Jc Lattes/Filipacchi, 1990), p. 30 (translated by the author).

2 Vijay Kranti, *Dalai Lama, the Nobel Peace Laureate, Speaks* (New Delhi: Centrasia Publishing Group, 1990), p. 75.

3 His Holiness the Dalai Lama, *Essential Teachings* (New Delhi: Ripa & Co., 1995), p. 15.

4 Kranti, *Dalai Lama, the Nobel Peace Laureate, Speaks,* p. 119.

5 Ibid.

6 Ibid., p. 177.

7 Le Dalaï-Lama and Jean-Claude Carrière, *La force du bouddhisme* (Paris: Robert Laffont, 1994), p. 182 (translated by the author).

8 Ibid., p. 181.

9 Ibid., p. 104.

10 Ibid., p. 25.

11 P. N. Chopra, *The Ocean of Wisdom: The Life of Dalai Lama XIV* (Ahmedabad: Allied Publishers, 1986), pp. 79–80.

12 Ibid., p. 78.

13 Kranti, *Dalai Lama, the Nobel Peace Laureate, Speaks*, p. 90.

14 His Holiness the Dalai Lama, *Essential Teachings*, p. 14.

15 Claude B. Levenson, *The Dalai Lama: A Biography* (London: Unwin Hyman, 1988), p. 264.

16 Kranti, *Dalai Lama, the Nobl Peace Laureate, Speaks*, p. 66.

17 Le Dalaï-Lama and Carrière, *La force du bouddhisme*, p. 15.

18 Levenson, *The Dalai Lama*, p. 212.

19 His Holiness the Dalai-Lama, *The Way to Freedom* (New Delhi: Harper Collins Publishers India, 1995), p. 94.

20 His Holiness the Dalai Lama, *Essential Teachings*, p. 17.

21 Mayank Chhaya, *Dalai Lama: Man, Monk, Mystic* (New York: DoubleDay, 2007), p. 166.

22 Gandhi, *All Men Are Brothers*, p. 165.

23 His Holiness The Dalai Lama, *The Four Noble Truths* (New Delhi: Harper Collins, 1997), p. 148.

24 Quoted in Bharati Puri, *Engaged Buddhism: The Dalai Lama's Worldview* (New Delhi: Oxford University Press, 2006), p. 41.

25 Anna Sebba, *Mother Teresa: Beyond The Image* (New York: DoubleDay, 1997), p. 19.

26 Quoted in Sebba, *Mother Teresa*, p. 157.

27 Quoted in Navin Chawla, *Mother Teresa* (London: Sinclair-Stevenson, 1992), p. 154.

28 Ibid., pp. 217–18.

29 Quoted in Sebba, *Mother Teresa*, p. 275.

30 King, *A Testament of Hope*, p. 242.

31 Ibid., pp. 240–1.

Conclusion

1 Gandhi, *My Nonviolence*, p. 32.

2 Thomas Merton, *The Pocket Thomas Merton*, ed. Robert Inchausti (Boston: New Seeds, 2005), p. 186.

3 Albert Camus, *Camus at Combat: Writing 1944–1947*, ed. Jacqueline Levi-Valensi, trans. Arthur Goldhammer (Princeton: Princeton University Press, 2006), pp. 275–6.

BIBLIOGRAPHY

Abu-Nimer, Mohammed, *Nonviolence and Peace Building in Islam: Theory and Practice*, Gainesville: University Press of Florida, 2003.

Ackerman, Peter and Christopher Kruegler, *Strategic Nonviolent Conflict: The Dynamics of People Power in the 20th Century*, Westport: Praeger, 1993.

Ackerman, Peter and Jack Duvall, *A Force More Powerful: A Century of Nonviolent Conflict*, New York: Palgrave Publishers, 2000.

Albert, David H., *People Power: Applying Nonviolence Theory*, Philadelphia: New Society Publishers, 1985.

Arendt, Hannah, *Between Past and Future*, New York: Penguin Books, 1993.

Arendt, Hannah, *On Revolution*, Harmondsworth: Penguin, 1990 [1963].

Arendt, Hannah, *On Violence*, New York: Harcourt Brace& Company, 1970.

Arendt, Hannah, *The Promise of Politics*, New York: Schocken Books, 2005.

Asher, Sarah Beth, Lester R. Kurtz and Stephen Zunes, eds, *Nonviolent Social Movements: A Geographical Perspective*, Malden: Blackwell Publishers, 1999.

Austin, Granville, *The Indian Constitution: Cornerstone of a Nation*, Delhi: Oxford University Press, 1966.

Awad, Mubarak, *Nonviolent Resistance in the Middle East*, Philadelphia: New Society Publishers, 1985.

Barnard, Rita, *The Cambridge Companion to Nelson Mandela*, Cambridge: Cambridge University Press, 2014.

Bartkowski, Maciej, ed., *Recovering Nonviolent History: Civil Resistance in Liberation Struggles*, Boulde: Lynne Rienner Publishers, 2013.

Beer, Michael, ed., *A Peace Team Reader: Nonviolent Third-Party Crisis Interventions by NGOs*, Washington, DC: Nonviolence International, 1993.

Bernstein, Richard J., *Violence: Thinking without Banisters*, Cambridge: Polity, 2013.

Bishop, Jim, *The Days of Dr. Martin Luther King, Jr.*, New York: G. P. Putnam Sons, 1971.

Bondurant, Joan V., *Conquest of Violence: The Gandhian Philosophy of Conflict*, Rev. edn, Berkeley: University of California Press, 1965.

Bose, N. K., *Selections from Gandhi*, Ahmedabad: Navajivan Publishing House, 1968.

Boserup, Anders and Andrew Mack, *War Without Weapons: Non-violence in National Defense*, Berlin: Schocken Books, 1975.

Brock, Peter, *Varieties of Pacifism: A Survey from Antiquity to the Outset of the Twentieth Century*, New York: Syracuse University Press, 1998.

Brock, Peter and Nigel Young, *Pacifism in the Twentieth Century*, Syracuse: Syracuse University Press, January 1999.

Brown, Judith M., *Gandhi: Prisoner of Hope*, New Haven: Yale University Press, 1989.

Burrowes, Robert J., *The Strategy of Nonviolent Defense: A Gandhian Approach*, Albany: State University of New York Press, 1996.

Camus, Albert, *Camus at Combat: Writing 1944–1947*, edited by Jacqueline Levi-Valensi, translated by Arthur Goldhammer, Princeton: Princeton University Press, 2006.

Camus, Albert, *Resistance, Rebellion and Death*, translated by Justin O'Brien, New York: Vintage, 1995.

Carrière, Jean-Claude and Le Dalaï-Lama, *La force du bouddhisme*, Paris: Robert Laffont, 1994.

Carson, Clayborne, *The Autobiography of Martin Luther King, Jr.*, New York: Grand Central Publishing, 2001.

Caute, David, *Fanon*, London: Fontana/ Collins, 1970.

Chawla, Navin, *Mother Teresa*, London: Sinclair-Stevenson, 1992.

Chenoweth, Erica and Adria Lawrence, eds, *Rethinking Violence: States and Non-State Actors in Conflict*, Cambridge, MA: MIT Press, 2010.

Chenoweth, Erica and Maria J. Stephan, *Why Civil Resistance Works: The Strategic Logic of Nonviolent Conflict*, New York: Columbia University Press, 2011.

Chernus, Ira, *American Nonviolence: The History of an Idea*, Danvers: Orbis Books, 2004.

Chhaya, Mayank, *Dalai Lama: Man, Monk, Mystic*, New York: DoubleDay, 2007.

Chopra, P. N., *The Ocean of Wisdom: The Life of Dalai Lama XIV*, Ahmedabad: Allied Publishers, 1986.

Cicovacki, Predrag, ed., *The Ethics of Nonviolence: Essays by Robert L. Holmes*, New York: Bloomsbury, 2013.

Cortright, David, *Gandhi and Beyond: Nonviolence for an Age of Terrorism*, Boulder: Paradigm, 2006.

Dalton, Dennis, *Mahatma Gandhi: Nonviolent Power in Action*, New York: Columbia University Press, 1993.

Einstein, Albert, *Ideas and Opinions*, New York: Crown Publishers, 1954.

Fanon, Frantz, *The Wretched of the Earth*, New York: Grove Press, 1963.

Finley, James S., ed., *Henry David Thoreau in Context*, Cambridge: Cambridge University Press, 2017.

Foley, John, *Albert Camus: From the Absurd to Revolt*, Stocksfield: Acumen, 2008.

Galtung, Johan, 'Principles of Nonviolent Action: The Great Chain of Nonviolence Hypothesis', in *Nonviolence and Israel/Palestine*, edited by Hawaii Institute for Peace, 13–33, Honolulu: University of Hawaii Institute for Peace, 1989.

Gandhi, Mahatma, *The Essential Writings*, Oxford: Oxford University Press, 2008.

Gandhi, Mohandas K., *All Men Are Brothers*, edited by Krishna Kripalani, New York: Continuum, 1980.

Gandhi, Mohandas K., *Gandhi, an Autobiography: The Story of My Experiments with Truth*, Boston: Beacon, 1993.

Gandhi, Mohandas K., *Harijan, Collected Works of Mahatma Gandhi*, New Delhi: Publications Division Government of India, 1999.

Gandhi, Mohandas K., *Hind Swaraj and Other Writings*, edited by Anthony J. Parel, Cambridge: Cambridge University Press, 1997. Contains the text of Gandhi's *Constructive Programme*.

Gandhi, Mohandas K., *My Nonviolence*, Ahmedabad: Navajivan Publishing House, 1960.

Gandhi, Mohandas K., *Non-Violent Resistance (Satyagraha)*, Mineola: Dover Publications, 2001.

Gandhi, Mohandas K., *Satyagraha in South Africa*, Ahmedabad: Navajivan Publishing House, 1950.

Gandhi, Mohandas K., *Satyagraha in South Africa*, Stanford: Academic, Reprints, 1954.

Gandhi, Mohandas K., *The Wit and Wisdom of Gandhi*, edited with an Introduction by Homer A. Jack, Boston: The Beacon Press, 1951.

Gandhi, Rajmohan, *Mohandas: A True Story of a Man, His People and an Empire*, New Delhi: Penguin-Viking, 2006.

Green, Martin, *Tolstoy and Gandhi, Men of Peace*, New York: Basic Books, 1983.

Gregg, Richard, *The Power of Nonviolence*, 3rd edn, Canton: Greenleaf Books, 1984.

Guha, Ramachandra, *Gandhi Before India*, Toronto: Random House Canada, 2014.

Hain, Peter, *Mandela: His Essential Life*, London: Rowman & Littlefield, 2018.

Hansen, Emmanuel, *Frantz Fanon: Social and Political Thought*, Ohio: Ohio University Press, 1977.

Hardiman, David, *Gandhi in His Time and Ours*, New York: Columbia University Press, 2003.

Harding, Walter, *The Days of Henry Thoreau: A Biography*, New York: Alfred Knopf, 1967.

Harding, Walter, ed., *Thoreau: A Century of Criticism*, Dallas: Southern Methodist University Press, 1965.

Harding, Walter, *A Thoreau Handbook*, New York: New York University Press, 1959.

Havel, Vaclav, *Disturbing the Peace: A Conversation with Karel Hvížďala*, New York: Alfred A. Knopf, 1990.

Havel, Vaclav, *Summer Meditations*, New York: Vintage Books, 1993.

Helvey, Robert, *On Strategic Nonviolent Conflict: Thinking about the Fundamental*, Boston: The Albert Einstein Institution, 2004.

His Holiness the Dalai Lama, *Essential Teachings*, New Delhi: Ripa & Co., 1995.

His Holiness the Dalai Lama, *The Four Noble Truths*, New Delhi: Harper Collins, 1997.

His Holiness the Dalai-Lama, *The Way to Freedom*, New Delhi: Harper Collins Publishers India, 1995.

Holmes, Robert L. and Barry L. Gan, eds, *Nonviolence in Theory and Practice*, Long Grove: Waveland Press, 2004.

Hutchins, Francis G., *India's Revolution: Gandhi and the Quit India Movement*, Cambridge, MA: Harvard University Press, 1973.

Iyer, Raghavan, ed., *The Moral and Political Writings of Mahatma Gandhi*, Oxford: Clarendon Press, 1986.

Juergensmeyer, Mark, *Gandhi's Way: A Handbook of Conflict Resolution*, Berkeley: University of California Press, 2002.

Keane, John, ed., *The Power of the Powerless: Citizens against the State in Central-Eastern Europe*, London: Routledge, 1985.

King, Coretta Scott, *My Life with Martin Luther King, Jr.*, New York: Holt, 1969.

King, Coretta Scott, *The Words of Martin Luther King, Jr.*, New York: Newmarket Press, 1987.

King, Jr., Martin Luther, *Strength to Love*, New York: Harper & Row, 1963.

King, Jr., Martin Luther, *Stride Toward Freedom*, New York: Harper and Row, 1958.

King, Jr., Martin Luther, *Where Do We Go From Here? Chaos or Community*, New York: Harper & Row, 1967.

King, Jr., Martin Luther, *A Testament of Hope: The Essential Writings of Martin Luther King, Jr*, edited by James Melvin Washington, New York: Harper & Row, 1986.

King, Jr., Martin Luther, *The Trumpet of Conscience*, New York: Harper & Row Publishers, Inc., 1968.

King, Mary, *Mahatma Gandhi and Martin Luther King, Jr.: The Power of Nonviolent Action*, Paris: UNESCO Publishing, 1999.

Kranti, Vijay, *Dalai Lama, The Nobel Peace Laureate, Speaks*, New Delhi: Centrasia Publishing Group, 1990.

Kumar, Mahendra and Peter Low, eds, *Legacy and Future of Nonviolence*, New Delhi: Gandhi Peace Foundation, 1996.

Kurlansky, Mark, *Nonviolence: The History of a Dangerous Idea*, London: Random House, 2007.

Levenson, Claude B., *The Dalai Lama: A Biography*, London: Unwin Hyman, 1988.

Levinas, Emmanuel, *Totality and Infinity*, translated by Alphonso Lingis, The Hague: Martinus Nijhoff, 1969.

Lodge, Tom, *Mandela: A Critical Life*, Oxford: Oxford University Press, 2006.

Mandela, Nelson, *Conversations with Myself*, Auckland: DoubleDay, 2010.

Mandela, Nelson, *Long Walk to Freedom*, London: Abacus, 1994.

Martin, Brian, *Social Defence, Social Change*, London: Freedom Press, 1993.

Martin, Brian, *Technology for Nonviolent Struggle*, London: War Resisters' International, 2001.

McCarthy, Ronald M. and Gene Sharp, with Brad Bennett, *Nonviolent Action: A Research Guide*, New York: Garland Publishing, 1997.

Merton, Thomas, ed., *Gandhi on Non-violence*, New York: New Directions, 1965.

Merton, Thomas, *The Pocket Thomas Merton*, edited by Robert Inchausti, Boston: New Seeds, 2005.

Myerson, Joel, ed., *The Cambridge Companion to Henry David Thoreau*, Cambridge: Cambridge University Press, 1995.

Nagler, Michael N., *The Nonviolence Handbook: A Guide for Practical Action*, San Francisco: Berrett-Koehler Publishers, 2014.

Nepstad, Sharon Erickson, *Nonviolent Revolutions Civil Resistance in the Late 20th Century*, Oxford: Oxford University Press, 2011.

Oates, Stephen B., *Let the Trumpet Sound*, New York: Harper, 1982.

Parekh, Bhikhu, *Colonialism, Tradition and Reform*, New Delhi: Sage Publications, 1999.

Parekh, Bhikhu, *Gandhi*. Past Masters Series, Oxford: Oxford University Press, 1997.

Parel, Anthony J., *Gandhi's Philosophy and the Quest for Harmony*, Cambridge: Cambridge University Press, 2006.

Parel, Anthony J. and Judith M. Brown, *The Cambridge Companion to Gandhi*, Cambridge: Cambridge University Press, 2011.

Randle, Michael, *Civil Resistance*, London: Fontana Press, 1994.

Sanbonmatsu, John, ed., *Critical Theory and Animal Liberation*, Lanham: Rowman & Littlefield, 2011.

Sebba, Anna, *Mother Teresa: Beyond the Image*, New York: DoubleDay, 1997.

Sharma, Anand, ed., *Gandhian Way: Peace, Nonviolence and Empowerment*, New Delhi: Academic Foundation, 2007.

Sharp, Gene, *From Dictatorship to Democracy: A Conceptual Framework for Liberation*, Boston: The Albert Einstein Institution, 1993. Available at http://www.aeinstein.org/.

Sharp, Gene, *Gandhi as a Political Strategist, with Essays on Ethics and Politics*, Boston: Porter Sargent Publishers, 1979.

Sharp, Gene, 'The Intifadah and Nonviolent Struggle', *Journal of Palestine Studies* 19, no. 1 (Autumn, 1989): 3–13.

Sharp, Gene, *The Politics of Nonviolent Action. Part One: Power and Struggle*, Boston: Porter Sargent, 1973.

Sharp, Gene, *The Politics of Nonviolent Action. Part Two: The Methods of Nonviolent Action*, Boston: Porter Sargent, 1973.

Sharp, Gene, *The Politics of Nonviolent Action. Part Three: The Dynamics of Nonviolent Action*, Boston: Porter Sargent, 1973.

Sharp, Gene, *The Role of Power in Nonviolent Struggle*. Monograph Series No. 3, Cambridge, MA: Albert Einstein Institution, 1990.

Sharp, Gene, *Social Power and Political Freedom*, Boston: Porter Sargent, 1980.

Sharp, Gene, *There Are Realistic Alternatives*, Boston: Albert Einstein Institution, 2003. Available http://www.aeinstein.org/wp-content/uploads/2013/09/TAR A.pdf.

Sharp, Gene, *Waging Nonviolent Struggle: 20th Century Practice and 21st Century Potential*, Boston: Porter Sargent Publishers, 2005.

Smith, Kenneth L. and Ira G. Zepp, *Search for the Beloved Community: The Thinking of Martin Luther King, Jr.*, Valley Forge: Judson Press, 1974.

Sophocles, *The Three Theban Plays*, New York: Penguin Books, 1982.

Tahmasebi-Birgani, Victoria, *Emmanuel Levinas and the Politics of Nonviolence*, Toronto: University of Toronto Press, 2014.

Terchek, Ronald J., *Gandhi: Struggling for Autonomy*, Lanham: Rowman and Littlefield, 1998.

Thoreau, Henry David, *The Higher Law: Thoreau on Civil Disobedience and Reform*, Princeton: Princeton University Press, 1973.

Thoreau, Henry David, *Walden*, Toronto: Ryerson Press, 1965.

Tolstoy, Leo, *The Kingdom of God and Peace Essays*, translated by Aylmer Maude, New Delhi: Rupa, 2001.

Tolstoy, Leo, *Writings on Civil Disobedience and Nonviolence*, Philadelphia: New Society Publishers, 1987.

Tutu, Desmond, *No Future Without Forgiveness*, New York: DoubleDay, 1999.

Vernier Palliez, Claudine and Auger Benjamin, *Le Dalai Lama - La Presence Et L'exil*, Paris: Jc Lattes/Filipacchi, 1990.

Wolpert, Stanley, *Gandhi's Passion: The Life and Legacy of Mahatma Gandhi*, New York: Oxford University Press, 2001.

Žantovský, Michael, *Havel: A Life*, London: Atlantic Books, 2016.

Zinn, Howard, ed., *The Power of Nonviolence: Writings by Advocates of Peace, Anthology*, Boston: Beacon Press, 2002.

Zunes, Stephen, Lester Kurtz and Sarah Beth Asher, eds, *Nonviolent Social Movements: A Geographical Perspective*, Oxford: Wiley-Blackwell, 1999.

INDEX